PLAYING
WITH
PURPOSE

Inside the Lives and Faith of
the NFL's Most Intriguing Personalities
Jared Allen, Colin Kaepernick, Drew Brees, and others

MIKE YORKEY

BARBOUR
PUBLISHING

Member of the
Evangelical Christian
Publishers Association

Printed in the United States of America.

CONTENTS

INTRODUCTION

Every now and then, I'm invited to speak in high school classrooms about the way media is changing the way we receive and consume information. I love to do a "show and tell" presentation with part of my collection of old newspapers dating back to November 11, 1918, the day World War I ended. One paper I always bring is the *San Diego Evening Tribune* from November 22, 1963.

Perhaps you recognize that famous date from a half century ago. That Friday, at Dealey Plaza in Dallas, Texas, President John F. Kennedy was assassinated. The killing set off a convulsive period of change and self-doubt in this country, and many say our national innocence died along with the thirty-fifth president of the United States.

I hold up the front page of the *Evening Tribune*—with its grainy photos of the presidential motorcade and the words "5th EXTRA" blaring across the top. "Does anyone know what the word *extra* means?" I ask the fresh-faced students. I reckon few, in this day and age, have ever read a real newspaper from cover to cover.

A sea of blank stares. I plow ahead.

"An *extra* is when the newspaper decides to print another

edition containing updates of catastrophic or significant events," I explain. "Back then, news wasn't on your fingertips like it is today. There was no Internet or twenty-four-hour news networks on cable TV. Instead, newspaper boys would walk along city sidewalks, yelling, 'Extra, extra, read all about it!' People had to buy a newspaper for ten cents to get the latest news."

The students look at me like I had just said that once upon a time kids didn't have video games. But I'm not done yet. Next, I hold up the *Evening Tribune* sports section from November 22, 1963. "What stands out to you?" I ask.

Looks of puzzlement. Several students throw out ideas, but they're not even close.

"Take a look at the biggest story of the day," I say. I point to the It's Here—Big Moment for the Preps headline running across the top of the sports section. "It's evident from the three big pictures accompanying this story that the San Diego high school football playoffs are in full swing. The lead article breathlessly talks about the 'greatest team in Kearny High history' clashing with 'the best Escondido High squad ever' at Balboa Stadium in downtown San Diego." Then I direct their eyes to the front-page starting lineups of six high school playoff teams and a staged photo of a helmetless El Capitan High player—like a marionette on a string—diving on a football.

"Now look at this story, which is much less prominent." I aim my finger at a smaller article about the San Diego Chargers' upcoming game against the Houston Oilers (today known as the Tennessee Titans) tucked away on the right-hand side of the sports section. Back in 1963, the Chargers-Oilers clash pitted two American Football League powers, and the Chargers played their home games in—you guessed it—Balboa Stadium, a humble amphitheater built in 1914 for the Panama-California Exposition and site of the 1963 San Diego high school playoffs. Bench seating, just like you'd see on any school campus.

Seeing baffled looks on the students' faces, I know it's time to connect the dots. "In other words, we can glean from this sports page that back in 1963, high school football was more important than pro football," I say.

A half century later, I doubt you'll find high school football getting top billing over the local pro team in *any* of the thirty-two cities with an NFL franchise. Professional football—the most popular sport in America and the most valuable and profitable sports business on the planet—rules the sporting roost. For an enterprise founded nearly a century ago inside an automobile showroom in Canton, Ohio, the National Football League has grown from its nascent leatherhead days into the most powerful cultural, social, and economic force in American sports.

How did this phenomenon happen? How did football surpass baseball as the "national pastime" in the 1970s?

I'd say the answer is easy: *television*. No other invention has reshaped our lives—or the way we spend our recreational time—than the ubiquitous TV. Football and wall-mounted flatscreens are an ideal match for our sedentary lifestyle and watch-rather-than-do culture. And it certainly helps that football is mostly played in the fall and early winter months when much of the country is driven indoors by inclement weather.

Whether you're having friends and loved ones over to

watch the Big Game in the man cave or getting your football fix with the NFL Network's RedZone Channel—which leaps from game to game at dizzying speeds to deliver the most exciting moments live as they happen—the leather recliner is the place to be on Sunday afternoons . . . as well as Sunday evenings, Monday nights, and Thursday nights. We love how twenty cameras break down the complexity of the sport and never tire of the clichés spouted by the announcing crew. (My favorite: "You don't want to put the ball on the ground," as if the running back has never heard a coach say that fumbling is bad, bad, bad.)

Football's demarcating line-of-scrimmage and coast-to-coast action translate well to rectangular, sixty-inch flat screens, especially now that games are transmitted in high definition so sharp you can tell if New England quarterback Tom Brady has any crumbs in his three-day beard. Blue lines of scrimmage, yellow first-down lines, red lines across the 20-yard line, and down-and-yardage graphics superimposed on the field keep millions of football fans' heads in the game. Cable-suspended, computer-controlled Skycams hover over huddles and bring video-game camera angles to live action as well as replays.

But where would televised football be without the instant replay, which not only enhances the viewing experience but also allows NFL teams to challenge referee decisions that went against them? Just as it's hard to imagine a time when high school football garnered more media play than pro football, it's also strange to think of televised football before instant replay.

Ten days after President Kennedy was laid to rest at

Arlington National Cemetery, instant replay was used for the first time. It happened on December 7, 1963, during the annual Army-Navy college game. Tony Verna, a twenty-nine-year-old CBS director, had produced numerous football telecasts from the production truck and knew all about the long lulls of action—players taking their sweet time returning to the huddles, coaches shuttling players in and out of the game, prolonged injury time-outs, and referees throwing flags and discussing what penalties to mete out. "You could eat a sandwich between plays," he said.

Verna had an idea: If he and his production crew could show big plays or touchdowns a *second* time, the broadcast team could fill some of those dead moments. The young CBS director devised a system that used audio tones to cue video-tape to the point just before the ball was snapped. After working out the kinks, Verna was ready to give "instant re-play" a try at the Army-Navy football game. A cameraman in the press box fed a 1,200-pound videotape machine images of Navy quarterback Roger Staubach—a godly man destined to fashion a Hall of Fame career with the Dallas Cowboys—and Army quarterback Rollie Stichweh when each signal caller was behind center.

Snags cropped up, and it wasn't until the fourth quarter that CBS technicians believed the newfangled videotape machine would actually work. After Army's Stichweh punched in a touchdown from the one-yard line, Verna immediately replayed the touchdown at full speed—a revelation that prompted play-by-play announcer Lindsey Nelson to scream into his microphone, "This is not live, ladies and gentlemen! Army did not score again!"

Okay, Nelson's words don't have the same gravitas as Alexander Graham Bell's first telephonic pronouncement— "Mr. Watson, come here. I want to see you"—but they were plenty dramatic. Today it would seem unimaginable to sit through a football game without savoring exciting plays from every angle—or having a review process for the zebras to "get it right" after a blown call.

Let's face it: NFL football is the best reality show on TV. (And NBC's *Sunday Night Football* is the highest-rated program for *all* primetime series.) Every week there are new storylines, plot twists, and endless strategy debates. In the NFL, the old cliché that on any given Sunday, any team can win any game contains more than a kernel of truth.

Fans tune in hoping their favorite team will win—but the game's unpredictability adds to the excitement. Egg-shaped footballs with pointed ends bounce and roll in crazy directions whenever they're dropped, fumbled, or ripped from a player's grasp. Add in the tipped passes, blocked punts, field goals clanging off goalposts, butterfingered ball carriers, long kickoff returns, blindside hits on quarterbacks, and Hail Mary passes into the end zone—just when you think you've seen it all—football delivers ever-changing, heart-pounding denouements that Hollywood could never script.

Predicting outcomes is a fool's errand. NFL prognosticators have a track record on par with your local weatherman— to pick the winners, they might as well throw darts at a poster board of team logos. "When it comes down to it, nobody really knows what's going to happen," said Denver Broncos cornerback Champ Bailey, "and everybody looks dumb one week and smart the next."

USING TECHNOLOGY IN A POSITIVE WAY

Call me an evangelist for the DVR.

The invention of the digital video recorder—which allows fans to record games for viewing later on—has changed the way I watch football *forever*. Now I'm free to view games whenever it's most convenient—in less than half the "live" time.

Let's talk specifics. I live in San Diego (in the Pacific Time Zone), so the "early game" on Sunday starts at 10 a.m. Whenever the Chargers travel to the East Coast to play, opening kickoff is usually right in the middle of church.

So do I play hooky from Pastor Dale's sermon? Nope. Now, as I set my DVR, there are no moral dilemmas. I can watch the Chargers play when I get home from church sometime between eleven and noon. The game is still going on, but that doesn't matter. My DVR will play back the opening kickoff and every subsequent play, while I fast-forward through the breaks. That's easy to do with football, which has set plays that start the action, unlike "continuous motion" sports like basketball and soccer. If I start watching my DVR before noon, I often catch up to the live action by the end of the game.

I *love* to fast-forward through the dead time that inspired Tony Verna to invent instant replay—while also skipping a blizzard of beer commercials and Cialis ads of middle-aged couples sitting in bathtubs overlooking the beach.

Really, the DVR allows me to redeem buckets of time. Instead of losing three-and-a-half hours watching an NFL game live, I can witness every play in about an hour—or a bit longer if I want to savor a close game. When the Chargers play at home with a 1 p.m. start time, I set my DVR to record the game while I do family stuff or pursue leisure activities outside, especially if we have a nice 70-degree day in December. (I loved typing that sentence, knowing how fortunate I am to live year-round in a mild Mediterranean climate.) Then I'll watch the game when it's convenient for me—like at 5 p.m. before dinner.

Of course, time-shifting NFL games only works when you don't know the final score. Maintaining that ignorance can be a challenge, especially if you're walking in the vicinity of sports bars and restaurants—or find yourself in a social situation where someone with an iPhone blares out, "I can't believe the Steelers beat the Chargers again!" You'll have to turn off the car radio, forget about going online, and not listen to any phone messages until the game is over. (*Hey, Mike! Did you see Philip Rivers work the two-minute drill to perfection?*)

But what about the "shared" experience of watching the Big Game with friends on a Sunday afternoon or evening? Sure, that certainly calls for watching a game as it happens, and during the lulls between plays I do what everyone does—eat and chat. And, of course, there are those annual Super Bowl parties, where we gather to watch not only the final game of the NFL playoffs, but the over-the-top halftime show and all those cleverly produced thirty-second advertisements that air during the bloated broadcast.

But many NFL games don't have to be watched live. I've been at friends' homes for games when we've hung out for perhaps the first quarter, letting the game record while we catch up on each other's lives and children, then start watching about an hour in and zip through the dead spots. It's nice being in control that way—as long as no one is looking at his smartphone!

I've been a DVR evangelist with missionary zeal for ten years and can't imagine what life was like *before* cable TV boxes came with hard drives. DVRs cost around $10 to $15 extra a month on your cable bill, but I can't think of a more family-friendly expense—or better way to successfully manage how much time you spend watching football on TV.

HOSANNAS FOR THE SPORT

Football is teamwork and common values in action. In order for an eleven-man offense or defense to be successful, players of varying size, strength, and talent must work together in a highly coordinated fashion. If anyone on the team doesn't follow his assignment to the letter, plays can turn south in a hurry. At the same time, though, players must be resourceful, making split-second decisions that are often the difference between winning or losing games.

Football offers something for everyone. If you like strategy, you can be the armchair quarterback who second-guesses the play calling all game long. If you like speed, you can marvel at receivers streaking up the sideline on a "go" route, racing defenders to the long, spiraling pass thrown with laser-like precision. If you like collisions, you can wince when runners are decked by burly linebackers or receivers are flattened after catching a pass in traffic.

Football is a truly democratic sport with a place for play-ers of differing skills and body builds. Heavyset dudes with massive bellies man the offensive and defensive lines; tall, whippet-like receivers and smaller, quicker cornerbacks—all with world-class speed—duel each other in the secondary; and adept, cerebral quarterbacks have only a few seconds to size up the defense prior to the snap and about the same amount of time to decide what to do once they get the ball in their hands. No other sport requires so many split-second decisions and different skill sets as football.

For an individual football player, the odds of making it to the National Football League are so miniscule that they defy belief. First, you start with the number of kids who play high school football, which was 1,071,775 in 2012, according to the College Sports Scholarships website. Of those prep players, only 61,252—about 5.7 percent—were good enough to play at some college level—FBS (Football Bowl Subdivision), FCS (Football Championship Subdivision), Division II, and Division III.

The jump from college football to the pros is much more daunting. Of the 13,612 seniors in college football in 2012, plus several dozen juniors who declare themselves eligible for the NFL draft, only 224 players are selected (seven rounds times thirty-two teams). To make a team's final 53-man roster at the start of the season, those newly drafted players must compete with returning players on the active roster, eight players on each team's practice squad, veterans cut from other teams, plus undrafted free agents. Only then can they say, "I play in the NFL."

You may wonder how *anyone* crashes the party. There are thirty-two NFL teams, each with 53-man rosters, meaning there are 1,696 active players in the NFL at any given time. So the progression goes like this:

- High school: 1,071,775 players
- College: 61,252 players
- The NFL: 1,696 players

In other words, if you're good enough to make your high school football team, you have about a .001 percent chance of playing on Sundays.

But let's say you're good enough to be among the 224 players drafted by NFL teams every April or to be signed to a free agent contract for training camp. (Teams can bring 90 players into camp.) What then?

Chris Reis, who played for the New Orleans Saints and is an answer to a trivia question—who recovered the onside kick at the start of the second half of Super Bowl XLIV in 2010?—said that stepping into an NFL locker room for the first time was a reality check.

THEY DON'T CALL IT NFL GAME SPEED FOR NOTHING

Ask any NFL rookie to tell you the biggest difference between college and pro football, and he's apt to describe how the game has sped up—players get off the line of scrimmage faster and zip by at warp-speed. There's no doubt that exceptional first-step swiftness and blazing speed are what it takes to play at the next level. If you want to make an NFL roster, you simply have to be faster than 99.995 percent of the rest of the population.

There's a name for this phenomenon: NFL game speed.

I've stood on my share of high school sidelines and have been fortunate enough to have received sideline passes for major college games as well as for an NFL game between the San Diego Chargers and the Oakland Raiders. Being *that close* to a professional game was an awesome experience.

Here's how I would describe the difference between the levels of speed in high school, college, and pro football. If a sweep came my way in a high school game, I'd prudently take a step or two back to avoid getting run over. When I was on the sidelines at the Rose Bowl for a game between UCLA and Oregon State, I hopped several steps back when a tailback ran around the edge and turned up the sideline I was on. The college players were considerably bigger and faster than the high school runts.

The difference in speed between college and pro football,

however, amazed me. When I was on the sidelines of Qualcomm Stadium for the Chargers-Raiders game, I nearly turned and ran for the grandstands when a running play came my direction—and so did everyone around me. Defensive backs materialized out of nowhere, and the way the players threw their bodies around with reckless disregard had me scurrying for cover.

Those NFL guys were flying—and I wasn't about to get hit!

Chris, an undrafted free agent, said that when he arrived at the Atlanta Falcons training camp a few years ago, no players welcomed him or offered to show him the ropes. It was clear to him that he was on his own. The other players, he felt, were conducting a "look" test: *Did he look like an NFL player? Did he have what it takes to beat out other players for a job playing football?* Because of the competitive, dog-eat-dog nature of the NFL culture, Chris could sense what the other players were thinking: *This guy is coming in to take my position, trying to take food off my table. I'm not going to help him.*

"That was really eye-opening to me," Chris told me. "I learned that the NFL was cutthroat. Guys were playing for themselves, and they were playing for the money—a completely different atmosphere than college football. Not that it was wrong, but it was a rude awakening."

Playing for money.

Millions of Americans greatly enjoy watching football, but there's a soft underbelly to the game that must be addressed, and it's the money in the game and the way players are paid. First of all, most NFL players enjoy very short careers and often leave the game with significant injuries that either shorten their lives or give them plenty of aches and pains for the next fifty years. For these reasons, I'm all for professional football players making as much as they can in the abbreviated time they draw NFL paychecks.

According to the NFL Players Association, the average professional football player's career lasts only 3.3 years, which is why the NFL is often called the "not for long" league. The NFL, however, says that the career of a player who makes an opening day roster as a rookie is closer to six years in length. Whether it's three years or six years, or something in between, many NFL players are looking for another line of work by the time they're twenty-six, a young age to be switching careers. The last time I checked monster.com, there weren't a whole lot of jobs out there with a starting salary of $405,000, the minimum NFL base salary in 2013.

That sizable sum clearly puts NFL rookies among the "1 percenters," but there's another issue few are talking about— the *way* these young men are paid to play a violent game. Every two weeks during the NFL season, players receive a paycheck for approximately one-eighth of their annual salary. In other words, the players are paid only in-season. The rest of the year, no paychecks.

Sure, there are exceptions in some contracts. The top players have built-in incentives and signing bonuses in their contracts that spread the money out, but, by and large, the rank-and-file NFL players are paid bi-weekly during the season—as stated in the league's Collective Bargaining Agreement (CBA).

Think about it: for all intents and purposes, NFL players receive all their yearly earnings over a period of seventeen weeks—and nothing the other thirty-five weeks of the year. In addition, all the money is stacked at the top of NFL rosters. Big-name quarterbacks like Joe Flacco, Aaron Rodgers, Matthew Stafford, Drew Brees, Peyton Manning, Tony Romo, Eli Manning, Philip Rivers, Matt Ryan, Tom Brady, Ben Roethlisberger, Sam Bradford, and Matt Schaub make eight-figure salaries (as in $10 million and up), while rookies, special teams guys, and backups make a fraction of those cap-busting salaries. The median NFL salary—meaning half make more and half make less—is $770,000, but a lot of young first- and second-year players are in the minimum salary range of $405,000 to $480,000 a year.

For the sake of argument, let's take that median salary of $770,000 and divide that amount by seventeen. This works out to about $45,294 each week during the season, and that's before Uncle Sam takes his pound of flesh. Most NFL players are young, single males in their mid-twenties, so you have to figure that the taxman (federal and state) withholds around 40 percent of that amount, or about $18,117. Take-home pay, in that case, would be around $27,177—just for that week. Since players are paid bi-weekly, that means players who are making the median salary receive a fat check for more than $50,000 every two weeks.

We've got a bye this weekend. Let's go to Vegas!

Or purchase a tricked-out Escalade. Or, if you're a San Diego Charger, party with your posse at the Stingaree nightclub in the Gaslamp Quarter, where the average bar tab is $1,300. Or give your friends "walking around" money. Or loan family members money that will never be repaid.

Paul Saber, a friend of mine who owns nearly twenty Panera Bread Co. restaurants in the San Diego area and has been a close advisor both to Franklin Graham of Samaritan's Purse and the Billy Graham Evangelistic Association, can only shake his head.

"Players, for the most part, are only paid during the course of an NFL season," Paul said. "Even for mature individuals, that's a very difficult thing. What has stuck out to me is that the NFL has put these kids in harm's way. They've created a system that almost plans for their failure. It seems to me that the NFL would say that it's in the players' best interest to protect the health and the wealth of these young men by paying them over a fifty-two-week period. In the real world, nobody pays you your annual salary over a seventeen-week period. The teacher's unions recognized thirty-five years ago that teacher's pay should be spread out over twelve months so that teachers can live within a yearly budget."

The in-season paycheck policy is a holdover from the early days of the NFL, when itinerant players for teams like the Canton Bulldogs, Rochester Jeffersons, and Rock Island Independents demanded to be paid cash on the barrelhead right *after* the game—since they couldn't be sure if their team would be financially solvent the following week during those barnstorming years.

It would seem that the NFL would realize that it's in everyone's best interest to protect the players by paying them over a fifty-two-week period instead of giving them huge chunks of money during the NFL season. Soon, very soon, these young men will be living in a real world where no employer pays them astronomical amounts—as compared with what the average American makes—over the course of a four-month season.

LOSING IT ALL

Let me illustrate why this NFL salary issue is personal to me.

I remember standing in the Chargers players' parking lot—fenced off from the fans—a decade ago. My family had become friends with Mike Riley, the Chargers' head coach at the time, and his wife, Dee. (We were in the same Bible study and our children attended the same Christian school.) After home games, we would wait with Dee and her children for Mike to come out of the locker room.

Coaches are always the last to leave the locker room, so we had plenty of time to watch the Chargers players greet their girlfriends, wives, and friends before stepping into their cars to exit the Qualcomm Stadium parking lot.

Three things stood out to me:

• the bling around their necks and on their fingers
• the size of their posses and hangers-on
• their extravagant cars, which ranged from high-end, limited production Mercedes Benz to accessorized Cadillac Escalades equipped with boom boxes whose heavy bass notes rattled the pavement

That makes for an expensive lifestyle, and I'm afraid very few of those players have any money left in the bank a decade later. Going broke is pandemic in the NFL: according to *Sports Illustrated*, 78 percent of NFL players are bankrupt or in financial distress just two years after they play their last professional football game. The money evaporates into thin air, just as Proverbs 23:5 (New Living Translation) says it would: "In the blink of an eye wealth disappears, for it will sprout wings and fly away like an eagle."

One of the saddest stories of an NFL player going broke

in recent memory is that of former Tennessee Titans quarterback Vince Young, who burned through $26 million in six years of professional football. He squandered $5,000 a week at a Cheesecake Factory restaurant feeding friends and who-knows-who during his rookie season, purchased 120 seats on a Southwest Airlines flight from Nashville to Houston so he and his posse (twenty in all) could have plenty of room to stretch out, and sued his financial advisors for misappropriating $5.5 million on a series of bad investments. By the start of the 2012 season, Young was out of football and out of money.

Sadly, tales like Vince Young's are all too common, but we shouldn't be shocked. These young men are handed five-figure and six-figure checks every two weeks during the NFL season but are expected to soberly manage this windfall with an eye toward the future. Even though they are praised as modern-day warriors, esteemed for their courage and ability to play with pain, and lend their considerable athletic gifts to an entertaining game that attracts the biggest audiences for any spectacle in America, they are far too often separated from their money for a variety of reasons.

Too many of these players are unable to maintain a proper perspective in a culture that showers them with fame and money. The few who do maintain a good perspective are often young men who have a unique vantage point that comes from being followers of Jesus Christ. These are players who recognize that being an NFL football player gives them a platform to glorify Christ and the encouragement to stay away from the off-the-field silliness and boorish behavior we often read about.

From what I've been told, there are usually five to fifteen players on each NFL team who are playing with purpose—Christian players who try to live in a way that honors their faith and points people to the Lord. You're going to read about some of these players in this NFL edition of *Playing with Purpose*. Some are marquee stars that everyone who follows the NFL knows about. Others are role players you may be reading about for the first time.

The players featured in this edition of *Playing with Purpose* possess attributes that can't be measured with a stopwatch or by how hard they hit the tackling sled. They don't necessarily want to be put up on a pedestal, but they recognize that football puts them in the public eye and that people watch their every move off and on the field, poised to take a photo with their iPhone. They are aware that today's social media—Facebook and Twitter—holds them accountable.

So enjoy this cast in *Playing with Purpose*, but be sure to pray for them and other Christian players in the NFL. The challenges these young believers face playing professional football are wide and deep. More than most of us, they are confronted with temptations to lust for the flesh and the things of the world. The siren calls that come with being a sports celebrity are alluring and addictive, and most of us have no idea what it's like to experience the attention and money they receive. Somehow, they still have to play football and live life with a healthy attitude toward God and the way He wants them to behave.

It's not easy to shake off the temptations that come like a would-be tackler, so we need to give them grace. While we can't often see their faces because of the protective padding and hard plastic helmets they wear, they are real people underneath all those safeguards, wired with the same emotions and thoughts as other human beings.

They play with a sword of Damocles suspended over their heads, and their careers hang by a thread—a dropped pass, a fumble, an ill-timed interception, or a missed field goal separates them from an unemployment line.

Author Stefan Fatsis, who was allowed to "try out" as a kicker for the Denver Broncos during training camp a few summers ago, said the players wanted him to correct the vast misperceptions about what they do. Fatsis wrote, "The players wanted me to understand that apart from Sundays, which are simultaneously terrifying and exhilarating, their working lives are a seemingly endless string of unpleasantness: injuries, reminders from coaches that their jobs are on the line, distrust of their bosses, disgust over being scheduled like preschoolers, and unfathomable psychological pressure."

That's why some players cope by hitting downtown clubs during the week. One NFL player told me that every Friday night before a home game, coaches hold their collective breath because they *know* a certain number of players will be drinking and driving until two and three in the morning. The results can be disastrous, as illustrated late in the 2012 season, when Dallas Cowboy defensive lineman Josh Brent was arrested and charged with intoxication manslaughter after the speeding car he was driving hit a curb and flipped, killing his teammate, practice squad linebacker Jerry Brown. The accident happened at 2:20 a.m., and Brent's blood alcohol content was 0.18, more than double the legal limit. Authorities said a man of his size would have to consume fourteen drinks to become that intoxicated.

Listen, we all fall short, and plenty of football fans and NFL players, when they first heard of Jerry Brown's death and Josh Brent's arrest, could have whispered, *There but for the grace of God go I.*

That said, playing with purpose isn't any easier than *living* with purpose. Sometimes it can feel like we're playing the game of life in thick, heavy mud up to our ankles.

The difference in our lives—including those of the men featured in this book—is that we have the Lord coaching us every step of the way. All we have to do is listen to Him and follow His lead.

When we do that, we'll score a touchdown every time.

1

COREY LYNCH:
SAFETY IN GOD'S HANDS

The Cincinnati Bengals slogged through a ho-hum season in 2007, finishing 7–9 and out of the playoff mix. But the team led the NFL in one dubious category: the number of players arrested since 2000.

During a nine-month stretch before the 2007 season, police collared *nine* Bengal players and gave them chain bracelets for offenses such as driving under the influence, drunk and disorderly conduct, resisting arrest, drunken boating, possession of marijuana, spousal battery, burglary and grand theft, and providing alcohol to teenage girls.

Bengals fans didn't know which section of the newspaper to turn to first: the sports pages or the police blotter. A joke circulated around the Queen City that went like this:

There are four Bengals in a car. Who's driving?
Answer: the sheriff.

Wide receiver Chris Henry was the poster child of this lawless bunch. He was arrested four times between December 2005 and June 2006—for possession of marijuana in northern Kentucky, carrying a concealed weapon in Florida, driving under the influence in Ohio, and letting minors drink alcohol in a hotel room he had rented in northern Kentucky. NFL commissioner Roger Goodell suspended Henry for the first half of the 2007 season for repeatedly violating the league's conduct policy.

A fifth arrest in the spring of 2008—after he was accused of punching an eighteen-year-old man in the face and breaking his car window with a beer bottle—scuttled the wideout's NFL career. The Bengals organization severed its relationship with Henry, declaring that his off-the-field conduct could no longer be tolerated. (The Chris Henry story ended tragically in 2009 when he fell out of the back of a pickup truck with his girlfriend behind the wheel during an alleged domestic dispute. Henry died from his injuries the following day.)

Bengals owner and team president Mike Brown, known around the league as "The Redeemer," was said to have a soft spot in his heart for talented miscreants—whom he signed at discount rates. For wayward players, he was the patron saint of second, third, fourth, and fifth chances, but his 2007 Bengals team was a microcosm of character issues around the NFL. As the Bengals prepared for the 2008 NFL draft, the coaching staff was on the lookout for players who wouldn't wind up with their mug shots in the local paper.

I would have loved being a fly on the wall during the predraft meetings that spring. I think I may have seen something like this:

Coach #1: What do you think of this Corey Lynch kid? Do we draft him?

Coach #2: I dunno. He played at a Division I-AA school—Appalachian State.

Coach #1: You mean the team that beat Michigan last year?

Coach #3: Yeah, the biggest upset in college football last season—maybe of all time. Lynch blocked the winning field goal to save the day. Nearly ran it back for a touchdown before his legs gave out.

Coach #1: But can he play at the next level? Not too many players make the jump from 1-AA to the NFL. I can count them on two hands.

Coach #3: We've checked this kid out. He was a three-time All-American safety at Appalachian State. Picked off 24 passes in his career, more than any safety on our board. I ran the film on him. Good size, great speed. He's got real ball skills.

Coach #1: Character issues?

Coach #3: Let me put it this way: he married Billy Graham's granddaughter a couple of months ago.

Coach #1: Billy Graham? The preacher?

Coach #3: One and the same. Must be a special kid to pass muster with the Graham family.

Coach #1: So do we take a chance on him?

Coach #3: I think we need a guy like Corey Lynch in the locker room. I say we give him a chance.

YEAR-ROUND SPORTS

Corey Lynch's unlikely passage to the NFL began in his hometown of Cape Coral, Florida, a suburb of Fort Myers. There was a lot of testosterone in the Lynch household growing up:

Corey was the oldest of Brian and Linda Lynch's four sports-crazy boys.

Depending on the time of the year, there was always a back-yard football scrimmage, pickup basketball game, or Wiffle ball home run contest going on. As the boys grew older, they participated in organized sports year-round, keeping Mom on a hamster wheel getting the boys where they needed to go.

Brian was a fireman who worked twenty-four-hour shifts and then took two days off before he was due back at the firehouse. Like many young fathers who found it tough to support a family with a stay-at-home mom on one salary, Brian earned extra money by moonlighting. Brian's second job was as a concrete contractor who specialized in pouring driveways and coating backyard decks and pool areas.

"I was the guy who was constantly putting ten pounds into a five-pound bag, so I needed Linda to coordinate everything," Brian said. "She did an amazing job getting the kids where they needed to go, doing the books for the concrete business, watching every game, attending every award banquet, and making sure we had home-cooked meals. She did all that with tremendous passion."

Brian and Linda believed passionately in Christian education, so they were willing to do whatever it took to put Corey and his younger brothers Calan, Colton, and Colby—the parents obviously had a "C" thing going—into a private Christian school. The monthly checks they wrote to Providence Christian (for kindergarten through eighth grade) and Evangelical Christian School (for the high school years) dwarfed their mortgage payment.

Brian loved coaching, so it was only natural that he would

be Corey's first coach when he signed up his five-year-old son for Pop Warner flag football. Corey, a running back and defensive back in those early years, was such a gifted athlete that when he was ten years old, a parent approached Brian after Corey shredded the field with long touchdown runs and made open-field tackles on defense.

"Your son is going to play on Sundays," the father predicted.

Brian mumbled his thanks, but seeing his son play in the NFL seemed as remote to him as . . . meeting Billy Graham one day. "I did not believe what that parent said, even though everyone could see that Corey was extremely talented," Brian said.

It was around this time—when Corey was in the elementary school years—that Brian decided to get real about his faith. He had been raised in a Christian home, knew Jesus Christ was his savior, and attended church fairly often, but he preferred to stay on the sidelines and not get into the game. "I was a busy young father with all those boys, but sometimes you take God's grace too lightly, and that was what I was like," Brian said. "I was the lukewarm Christian that the Bible talks about, the type that Jesus said He would spew out of His mouth. I needed to make a transformation in my life, and I did."

Corey soon began to notice differences in his dad. When Corey got up in the morning, he would see his father reading the Bible at the kitchen table. Brian also made sure the family was more regular about going to church on Sunday mornings. "I started to see my father live out his faith," Corey said, "and that was huge."

Corey's father let it be known that Christ was No. 1 in his life. Witnessing how his dad made these changes and became the spiritual leader in the home deeply impacted Corey and gave him an example of what following Christ whole-heartedly and with passion looked like.

Brian became a man of his word, and that applied to the way things ran inside the home. "If I reminded the boys that they were told to clean up their rooms before playing with a board game, then that's what they had to do," Brian said. "But if they played their game before cleaning up their messy rooms, I would fold the game up and take it away. There were no second chances.

"Kids need absolutes in life and the assuredness of right and wrong. When I explained what was wrong and unacceptable, they learned that there were consequences to their actions. My boys became very aware. Corey and his brothers knew that I meant what I said, and there would be no deviation in that."

One of the rules Brian instituted was this: the boys were not allowed to spend the night at their friends' homes. He explained that he could not control how other families lived their lives or what they allowed their children to do or watch, so he didn't want to leave them under the control and guidance of others—even for a night. The boys' friends, however, could spend the night at the Lynch house any time they wanted.

"My boys thought that was the dumbest thing they had ever heard, but if you were to ask Corey about it today, he'd say, 'We'll probably do the same around our house,'" Brian said.

The intentional parenting took root. When Corey was twelve years old, Brian began to notice that his oldest son was standing up for his faith in ways that left him shaking his head in admiration. "When kids got nasty, Corey left the conversation. When they told vulgar jokes, he walked away. Corey was a kid who was willing to stand his ground for what he felt Christ was in his life," Brian said. "There was an aura about him."

As Corey was about to enter his high school years at Evangelical Christian School, the football team was just starting its third season. The young program had taken its lumps, as can be expected for any start-up team.

"I don't want to go to ECS," Corey said to his father as he entered the ninth grade. "The football team is terrible."

Corey could be excused for wanting to look for greener fields and better competition. Even at a young age, he was driven to succeed. When he was in eighth grade, he decided he wasn't going to drink any more soft drinks because he knew they weren't good for his health. Instead of eating sweets as a treat, he'd grab a piece of fruit.

Corey was determined to become the best football player he could be, but Evangelical Christian, with a miniscule high school student body of 185 students, was a tiny high school that played in the lowest classification in the state of Florida — 1A. (Depending on the size of the school, Florida high schools played in divisions from 1A all the way up to 6A.)

Brian held up his hands at his son's protestations. "Listen, if things don't work out, we'll transfer," he told Corey.

Like most high schools in the Fort Myers area, Evangelical Christian didn't have a freshman football team. That's because the ninth graders there seemed to gravitate toward the City League, which played a thirteen-game schedule that was far more competitive than high school freshman ball. Corey played on a City League team and gained valuable playing experience.

Brian was intensely interested in giving his son the greatest chance to succeed, so when Corey was about to enter his sophomore year in high school, he applied for an assistant coaching position at Evangelical Christian, which was rubber-stamped for approval. "It wasn't like ECS was a big program," Corey said. "Dad had tons of coaching experience and had been my coach pretty much since I started playing football in kindergarten."

Corey understood the sacrifices his father made just to be on the practice field. "During 'heaven week' at our summer training camp, I remember Dad getting up at 4 a.m. and doing concrete work from 5–7 a.m., then he'd be with us from eight in the morning until three in the afternoon," Corey said. "When we were done, he'd go help out at my brother's Pop Warner practice from five until seven o'clock. He'd be exhausted, but he loved every minute, even though he lost money because he couldn't do as much concrete work on the side. He also juggled his work schedule at the fire station to be at all my games. If he couldn't switch days off, he'd use vacation time."

MAKING DEPOSITS

Brian was promoted to head coach at Evangelical Christian for Corey's junior and senior years, and having a father coaching a son who was head-and-shoulders better than everyone else on the field made for an interesting dynamic. Should Brian coach his son "hard"—verbally reprimand him when he made a mistake—and show the other players that he played no favorites? Or should he treat Corey the same as everyone else and not make an example out of him?

First of all, both father and son agree that Brian was known for, well, raising his voice when he saw something he didn't like on the practice field.

You're not working hard!

You've got to do a better job!

Get your butt to work, or I'm going to put one of the other boys in your position!

Brian wasn't averse to stepping inside a player's personal space—say within six-to-eight inches from his facemask—and screaming that it was put-up-or-shut-up time.

"I could be extremely rude," Brian said. "I yelled things like, *I've had all I can take of you! You either get the job done, or you can go directly to the bench—and I mean now!* I always yelled at full volume."

But shouting at players only gets a high school football coach so far, Brian said, because coaching is a lot like having a bank account: you have to deposit money every now and then (say something encouraging) before you make a withdrawal (get in his grill). Brian said that deposits of "Good job!" and "Way to fight!" and "Atta-boy!" had to be greater than the withdrawals of "What happened? You blew that coverage!"

"If deposits aren't greater than withdrawals, then your bank account is going to run empty, and bad things will happen out on the field," Brian said.

During Corey's sophomore season, Brian was guilty of overdrafting his bank account with his son. "Dad had yelled at me on the football field, and it rubbed me the wrong way," Corey said. "I reacted by shutting down, and it wasn't a good situation. Eventually, we talked about it at home, and he changed the way he coached me."

Good thing, because Corey went on to be a one-man wrecking crew at Evangelical Christian. He rushed for 3,000 yards and was a ball hawk on defense, snaring 31 interceptions during his three-year high school career. He was brilliant on the football field, twice earning All-State Class 1A honors, and in the classroom, where he was a National Honor Society student who excelled in his science classes, especially physics.

Major Division I football programs rarely recruit players from small high schools, and Corey was no exception. The service academies—Army and Navy—showed mild interest, but when Princeton stepped up, Brian and Linda were in seventh heaven. To have their son gain entrance to an elite Ivy League college—through playing football—would be icing on the cake. But before Corey could play for Princeton, he had to win admission on academic merit and his SAT scores.

The Princeton opportunity was still up in the air when Corey's senior season was over. In early December, he was invited to play in the 2002 John Carrigan Rotary South All-Star Classic, which brought together the best graduating seniors in the Fort Myers area so they could showcase their talents for college recruiters one last time.

Chris Moore, a linebackers coach at Appalachian State University in Boone, North Carolina, was in West Florida that week on a recruiting trip. Moore was looking for players up and down the Sunshine State who—to put a nice spin on it—the major colleges had overlooked. Moore was the son of Appalachian State head coach Jerry Moore, who had presided over the program since 1989.

In the John Carrigan All-Star game, Corey was told to cover a 6-foot, 6-inch receiver "like white on rice"—a tall order since he gave up six inches of height. From all accounts, though, Corey played spectacularly in coverage, although he still remembers going for an interception and getting his hands on the ball, only to have it torn out of his outstretched arms by the taller receiver, who ran the ball in for a touchdown.

After the game, Brian jogged onto the field to congratulate his son for his excellent play and to commiserate about the bad luck on the near interception. Suddenly, Coach Moore joined them and made eye contact with Brian. "Is there any chance your son would want to go to Appalachian State?" he asked.

"Where's Appalachian State?" Brian asked.

"Boone, North Carolina."

"Where's Boone, North Carolina?"

Father and son would soon find out. Within a couple of weeks, Brian and Corey were on a plane to visit Appalachian State, which suitably impressed them both. They personally saw how Jerry Moore had built the Mountaineers into a perennial Division I-AA powerhouse and learned that Appalachian State scheduled games against major college teams each season.

Still, Mom and Dad couldn't get Princeton out of their minds. In their minds, having their son attend an Ivy League school sounded like an extraordinary opportunity. Corey needed the right score on his SAT II test to win acceptance to Princeton, however, so he took the test in late December. When the results came back two weeks later, he found out he was short of the mark.

The next SAT II test was in the middle of February, but National Signing Day—the day high school recruits are expected to sign national letters of intent with the schools of their choice—was the first Wednesday of that same month. There would be no way Corey and the family would learn whether Corey's SAT results were good enough for admission to Princeton until early March, a month after National Signing Day.

Appalachian State was the bird in the hand and would not wait, which made Brian's prayer time very interesting. "You should have heard my prayers," Brian said. "They were pretty one-sided and almost comical in the way I tried to manipulate God."

Lord, You know what a great school Princeton is, and that Princeton is a better school than Appalachian State. Lord, You know that Corey's opportunities at Princeton would be so much more vast and expansive than going to a school in Boone, North Carolina. Lord, if You want Corey to play for Princeton, You are welcome to make this dream happen for my son.

As for Corey, he was going with the flow. When National Signing Day came around, Appalachian State was still the only school that put an offer on the table. If this Division I-AA school wanted him to play football and was willing to pay for his tuition, books, and living expenses, then Appalachian State was where he would go.

It looks like the Lord knew what He was doing when He closed the door on Princeton and opened up another in the Blue Ridge Mountains of North Carolina. You see, Boone was also the home of Samaritan's Purse, which was headed by Franklin Graham, whose famous father and mother lived in a mountainside log cabin outside of town.

Franklin and his wife, Jane, also had a daughter who was a year younger than Corey. Named after her mother, her nickname was Cissie.

BLOCK THAT KICK!

The highlight of Corey's college career at Appalachian State can be summed up in one word: Michigan. We'll get to how David slew Goliath with a smooth stone in a bit, but there are some things about Appalachian State that you might find interesting.

Back in 1978, the National Collegiate Athletic Association (NCAA) split Division I football teams into two divisions: I-A and I-AA. The I-A schools, which number around 110, include the names every college football fan has heard of: University of Alabama, Louisiana State University, Notre Dame, University of Southern California, and Stanford, to name just a few.

Division I-AA schools are usually smaller schools with smaller football programs, smaller stadiums, and, hence, smaller profiles. Think of schools like William and Mary, Eastern Illinois, Marshall, Montana and Montana State, and Appalachian State. In the past thirty-five years, Division I-A and Division I-AA teams have played more than 2,200 times, and Big Brother has won 82 percent of the time.

Don't get the idea that there isn't some good football played at the I-AA level, which became known as the Division I Football Championship Subdivision (FCS) in 2006, Corey's junior year. You've probably heard of Tony Romo (Eastern Illinois) of the Dallas Cowboys and Joe Flacco (University of Delaware) of the Baltimore Ravens, both great quarterbacks who came out of the FCS. Vincent Jackson, the All-Pro receiver with Tampa Bay, played at the University of Northern Colorado. Jared Allen, the Minnesota Vikings defensive end who's also featured in *Playing with Purpose*, earned his stripes at Idaho State. According to my research, there were 148 FCS players in the NFL during the 2012 season, or about one in twelve players, or 8 percent of the team rosters.

From his first training camp prior to the 2003 season,

Corey turned out to be an impact player at Appalachian State. He won the starting job at free safety before the second game of the season and would go on to start every game for the next five seasons (when he wasn't injured). Corey was the only freshman named All-Southern Conference during the 2003 season, thanks to six interceptions and four fumble recoveries.

The game day atmosphere at Kidd Brewer Stadium made Saturday afternoons special for the Mountaineers. The entire town rallied around its football team, but Boone was and remains one of the few college towns where the students outnumber the residents. Around 17,000 students attend Appalachian State, while nearly an equal number reside inside the city limits year-round. Tucked in a picturesque valley and surrounded by the heavily forested Blue Ridge Mountains, Boone's small town atmosphere, traditional downtown layout, and leafy residential streets create an inviting place to spend your college years.

Since Boone *is* Appalachian State and Appalachian State *is* Boone, having a powerhouse football team nearly every season is a big deal to the students and residents alike. One of the football team's big boosters was Jane Graham, the wife of Franklin Graham, Billy's son and president of Samaritan's Purse, an international Christian relief and evangelism organization that provides spiritual and physical aid to victims of war, poverty, natural disaster, and disease.

Jane was a good friend of head coach Jerry Moore and an unofficial "team mom." Over the years, Jane took an interest in the young men on the football team and enjoyed it when they dropped by the house. Like her mother-in-law, Ruth Bell Graham, Jane had an enormous heart for young people and reached out to those who were away from home for the first time.

One of those players was Corey, who, during his sophomore year, fractured his left elbow returning a punt in the second game of the season. This nasty injury required surgery that left a long scar on the inside of his left arm. During rehab, Corey had to wear a sling for several months.

"How are you doing your laundry?" Jane asked.

"With one arm," Corey replied. "I'm managing."

"Why don't you bring your dirty clothes and things over to the house? I'll do your laundry for you."

Hanging around the Graham house led to the inevitable introduction of Franklin and Jane's fourth child and only daughter, Cissie. She was attending Liberty University in Lynchburg, Virginia, a four-hour drive away, but she often came home on weekends.

Sparks didn't fly right away in any romantic sort of way, however. Cissie thought Corey was another one of those boisterous, burping, and a bit rude football players who seemed to congregate at the Graham home.

KNACK FOR THE BALL

Because Corey's season-ending elbow injury happened in just the second game of the 2004 season, he was able to successfully petition the NCAA for a medical redshirt and another year of college football eligibility. During his second "sophomore" season, Corey shined like a bright star in the Mountaineer secondary, leading the team with six interceptions and winning All-American accolades.

It's a big understatement to say that the Mountaineers

had a pretty good season in 2005, after Coach Moore junked the I formation for a no-huddle spread offense to mix things up. Sure, the team lost to Division I-A schools University of Kansas and LSU, "guarantee games" played on the road that offered big payouts to the visitors. But the Mountaineers kept winning against teams their own size and qualified for the Division I-AA playoffs. While the major college teams played in the BCS bowl system, Division I-AA *did* have a playoff structure in place, with sixteen teams qualifying for post-season play that year. (BCS football teams will begin using a four-team playoff system with the 2014 season.)

In the 2005 playoffs, Appalachian State beat Lafayette and Southern Illinois in the first two rounds, avenged an early-season loss to Furman in the semifinal, and tripped up Northern Iowa 21–16 in the national championship game before 20,236 fans in Chattanooga, Tennessee and a nationwide TV audience looking in on ESPN2. The Division I-AA football championship was a source of considerable pride for those who called Boone their home.

The Mountaineers backed up their national championship in 2006 by going 14–1 and winning the first-ever FCS championship. The only blemish on their record was a season-opening 23–10 road loss to North Carolina State.

The 2007 Mountaineer season, Corey's senior year, started with another tussle against the big, bad Michigan Wolverines. Appalachian State was expected to come into Ann Arbor's Michigan Stadium and play the role of sacrificial lamb against the fifth-ranked FBS team in the country—in other words, be a "worthy opponent" and then succumb to the inevitable 56–14 thrashing at the hands of a big-time program.

Playing Michigan before 109,218 true-blue Wolverine fans certainly carried an intimidation factor. Actually, there were several hundred Appalachian State fans in attendance, including Brian and Linda Lynch, who boarded a 6 a.m. flight that morning at Southwest Florida International Airport in Fort Myers. (Brian had to coach Evangelical Christian's football team Friday night.)

Brian and Linda connected in Charlotte, made their flight to Detroit, raced to the taxi stand—there was no time to rent a car—and sweated out twenty highway-clogged miles to Ann Arbor. Holding hands, they ran from their drop-off point to their seats in the last row of the humongous Michigan Stadium, barely making it in time for the noon kickoff.

What Corey's parents witnessed made the long trip as enjoyable as it gets. During the first half, the Mountaineers' wide-open spread offense resulted in several big pass plays that put them on top 28–17 at intermission.

Brian had seen enough football games in his lifetime, however, to know that Appalachian State didn't have the horses to stay with Michigan in the second half. To stay competitive, Coach Moore subbed only one player on defense and just a couple on offense. Corey didn't normally play all the special teams, but against Michigan, he was on the field for all punts, punt returns, kickoffs, and kickoff returns.

Even though Michigan could throw in fresh reinforcements at will, Appalachian State wouldn't go away in the second half and nursed a 31–26 lead into the fourth quarter. In crunch time, though, Michigan came back late in the game and scored on a 54-yard run by running back Mike Hart to go up 32–31. The two-point conversion attempt failed, meaning the Mountaineers needed a field goal to retake the lead.

What happened next was heart-stopping football at its best. The Mountaineers had been unable to move the ball for most of the second half, but with just 1:37 to go, quarterback Armanti Edwards led his team on a 69-yard drive—with no time-outs— that resulted in a 24-yard field goal with just 27 seconds left. You'd think that would be enough to win the game, right?

Not if you were a Big Blue fan. Even though Appalachian State clung to a 34–32 lead, everyone in the Big House knew the script was being written for a Michigan field goal that would allow the home team to escape with a 35–34 victory. Sure enough, a 46-yard pass play—how did *that* happen?— took the ball down to the Mountaineers' 20-yard line with six seconds to go. Time for a 37-yard field goal to win the game and send the Mountaineers home with a bitter defeat.

But what transpired in the next few seconds changed Corey's life. As the ball was snapped, he charged through a gap in the Michigan line and blocked Jason Gingell's attempt, scooped up the ball without breaking stride, and set off for the end zone. "I had knots in my calves, and my legs started shivering," Corey said. He nearly made it to the house in the Big House, but Gingell tackled him at the 5-yard line as time expired. Seconds later, the entire Appalachian State team, delirious with happiness for registering one of the greatest upsets in college football history, fell on top of Corey.

Suddenly, Corey's name was on the lips of ESPN pundits. He was the player *Sports Illustrated* writer Austin Murphy featured in the magazine's cover story, "All-time Upset." After the season-opening victory, Appalachian State went on to have another banner season, finishing 13–2 and bringing home another FCS Championship, defeating Delaware and future NFL quarterback Joe Flacco in the season finale.

Corey only had one more date circled on his 2007 calendar—a wedding date with Cissie Graham on New Year's Eve.

A LONG CAR DRIVE

When Brian heard that Corey had been hanging out at the home of Franklin and Jane Graham and had met their cute daughter, who was around his age, he had a question for his son.

"Are you going to be dating that Graham granddaughter?" he asked.

"Not likely," Corey replied with a typical shrug of his shoulders. In the vernacular of the day, he wasn't into her, even though she was certainly a beautiful young woman worthy of being crowned Queen of the Shenandoah Apple Blossom Festival in Winchester, Virginia.

Cissie was hearing a similar question from her mom, who liked Corey and thought her daughter should get to know him better.

"Mom, I'm not impressed with that guy," she said. "We're complete opposites."

But the two were certainly on friendly terms, and Corey hung out at the Graham house a lot. What slowly attracted Cissie to Corey was that he had an uncompromising faith that reminded her of her father. She knew that Corey was one of the leaders of a team Bible study that got bigger and bigger every year. She had witnessed the stands for Christ he had taken, like the time when the team used a pregame chant that included foul language and Corey said, "We won't do this chant again." She accompanied Corey and several teammates when they would step onto the field at Kidd Brewer Stadium the night before home games and pray for every player.

Attraction bells were starting to ring for Corey as well, but he made a smart move: he didn't chase after her. In football terms, he dropped back into coverage and kept an eye on her. There was no all-out blitz of attention.

He waited to make his move and, like a safety who knows how to wrap up a runner in the flat, he wasn't going to let her go. They started dating in the summer of 2005, after Cissie finished her freshman year at Liberty University. Her plans were to take the fall semester off and participate in a Samaritan's Purse project in Thailand for several months—time that would also give her a chance to deal with a serious eating disorder she had said held her captive.

After two weeks of dating that summer, shortly before Cissie flew off to Bangkok, Corey invited her to his Fort Myers home to spend some time with his family. Twelve hours in a car together was a good way for the two young people to get to know each other. So was taking romantic strolls on the beach.

While Cissie worked at an orphanage in Thailand, absence made their hearts grow fonder. Caring for the needs of the "least of these" helped Cissie realize that her eating issues, while they were a serious health problem, couldn't compare with the desperate needs she witnessed at the orphanage. She was in Thailand to serve the Lord, and that's when she turned a corner and started to heal.

Cissie surprised Corey when she returned from Thailand early to watch him play in the 2005 Division I-AA playoffs— which culminated in Appalachian State winning the first of three consecutive national championships.

"I'm in awe, standing back there, and Favre looks over to my left, motions to his wide receiver, and then I read his lips: *Just go on the outside*," Corey said. "In other words, make a 'go' route up the sideline."

"I wondered, *Did he just say what I thought he just said?* This had to be a trick. He was testing me. The ball was snapped, and I started backpedaling. He looked over to his receiver, so I edged closer, but all the time I was thinking Favre was trying to get me to bite on something. Then he reared back and launched the ball high into the air. It *was* a go route up the sideline. I made a bead on the ball and nabbed my first NFL interception on Brett Favre. How cool was that?"

I'd say *really* cool, but Corey's rookie season ended after seven games when he injured his knee and was placed on injured reserve.

Like all injured players, Corey continued to collect his rookie minimum salary of $295,000. Coming into the NFL, Corey understood that he could be cut at any time and *poof*—the checks would disappear. After he signed his contract and received his modest sixth-round signing bonus, he read one of Christian financial counselor Dave Ramsey's books on being a good steward of money. Since NFL careers, to quote English political philosopher Thomas Hobbes, are "nasty, brutish, and short," he was determined that he and Cissie would live frugally and husband their resources for a rainy day.

TO THE RESCUE

In the summer of 2009, the Bengals organization allowed an NFL Films camera crew—working for the HBO show *Hard Knocks*—unfettered access to the team during training camp at

Georgetown College in Georgetown, Kentucky. Cameras and microphones were allowed into the players' and coaches' meeting rooms, training facility, dorms, and practice fields as they followed the daily lives of the ninety players in training camp.

Talk about a close-up.

Hard Knocks, which the NFL billed as the "first sports-based reality series," was known for choosing teams mired in controversy and populated with colorful players. The Bengals certainly fit that bill. One storyline belonged to a 6-foot, 5-inch receiver who had recently changed his last name from Johnson to Ochocinco, Spanish for 8–5, which matched his uniform number.

Chad Johnson/Ochocinco was a high-maintenance diva who marched to the beat of his own drummer. His end zone celebrations after catching a touchdown pass were of the "Can you top this?" variety: Irish step-dancing like a "Riverdance" performer; falling to one knee and proposing to a Bengals cheerleader; performing CPR on a football; and yanking an orange pylon from the corner of the end zone and using it to "putt" the football toward an imaginary hole, then punctuating the act with a Tiger-like fist pump. Some of the over-the-top Ochocinco touchdown celebrations merited fines from the NFL.

Reality shows like *Hard Knocks* love "casting" characters like Ochocinco, but then the director learned about a heart-tugging story involving a second-year player named . . . Corey Lynch.

The segment featured on *Hard Knocks* told the following account:

Father's Day, June 21, 2009. Corey and Cissie were driving from Cincinnati to Fort Myers—a distance of 877 miles—following the completion of organized team activities (OTAs). About 45 minutes into their trip, they were heading into Lexington, Kentucky, when Corey noticed a red van 75 yards ahead of him. A car suddenly swerved in front of the van, cutting off the vehicle. The van lurched to the left and onto the grassy meridian, then the driver overcorrected and the vehicle jerked to the right and across two lanes of interstate, somehow missing other vehicles and semi-trucks on the road. But the van kept right on going, launching off the interstate and down a steep embankment nearly 300 feet deep.

Corey and Cissie watched in horror as the van flipped a half-dozen times and tumbled down the hill, coming to a rest on its roof with the wheels pointing to the sky.

As the son of an emergency first-responder, there was no doubt what Corey would do next. He quickly pulled off onto the shoulder, and Cissie watched as he sprinted toward the accident scene in his sandals, nearly slipping several times as he made his way down the embankment. Two other Good Samaritans followed in his steps.

Corey expected to find twisted bodies and see death. Instead, he saw a six-year-old boy climbing out of a broken window, bloodied but all right. An older sister, age twelve, was bleeding and working her way out of the wreckage.

After settling the children, Corey and the two other men worked to free their father, who was upside down in the driver's seat, legs wrapped around the steering column. They freed him quickly, and he appeared okay, but the older woman in the passenger's seat was hanging upside down, held up by her seat belt. The way she hung—lifeless, still and unmoving—could mean only one thing: she was a goner.

"There was no way she could have made it," Corey said. "She looked dead to me."

Then Corey saw a couple of moving fingers and a labored attempt to breathe. It was apparent to him that the woman's body was crushing her windpipe, keeping her lungs from filling with air.

"Save my grandma!" one of the kids cried out.

Without regard for his personal safety, Corey climbed through the broken glass and into the van to free her. He finally located the release button for the seat belt, which he pressed. The woman immediately fell in a heap. Corey summoned his strength and pulled her out of the van. He and the others tended to her until paramedics arrived on the scene.

Six weeks later, Cynthia Brennan-Ritchie, a fifty-two-year-old grandmother, visited the Bengals training camp with her family. She was wearing a bulky neck brace and not moving very quickly. The accident had broken the vertebrae in her neck and back.

Upon seeing Corey again, Mrs. Brennan-Ritchie was visibly emotional, and the *Hard Knocks* crew recorded fascinating footage of her thanking Corey for being the angel who had saved her life.

Corey, still in his uniform, had taken a break from practice to visit with the family, who implored him to get back on the field with his teammates. "No, I'd rather hang out with you guys," Corey said, which touched the family.

Later, Corey said that God had blessed him by putting him in a situation to help. "I don't want to pat myself on the back," he said, "but this made me realize that I don't want to be the guy who puts his car in park and watches, or the guy who drives past. The guy who cut the van off? He never stopped.

"It's the brevity of life, you know? The Bible says that life is but a vapor. We drive three thousand-pound cars around every day. It kind of wakes you up and makes you think about life longer and harder. Life is but a vapor."

TAMPA BAY AND SAN DIEGO BECKON

After saving Mrs. Brennan-Ritchie's life, Corey didn't make the 53-man Bengals roster in 2009 but was placed on the practice squad, which made him eligible to be picked up by other teams. The Tampa Bay Buccaneers—his hometown team—brought him aboard three weeks into the season, and Corey saw plenty of action and played well on defense and special teams. Best of all, his parents and his brothers got to attend all his home games.

In 2010, Corey played in every game and performed skillfully for a Tampa Bay team that failed to make the playoffs but turned things around with a 10–6 record. (The team had won just three games in 2009.) The following season, 2011, Corey played in all sixteen games, but the Bucs' fortunes sank like a pirate ship. Tampa Bay lost its last ten games that year and finished 4–12, leading to the firing of the coaching staff. Corey's contract was also up, meaning he was a free agent.

Meanwhile, the San Diego Chargers had hired Rich Bisaccia, Tampa Bay's special teams coach for nine seasons who knew of Corey's work ethic. When Coach Bisaccia reached out to Corey and asked him to come to San Diego, the first thing Corey said was, "My wife will be happy."

Cissie had spent a couple of weeks in San Diego in May

2003, when her grandfather did one of his last evangelistic crusades. A woman named Dianne Saber—her husband, Paul, worked closely with Franklin Graham on various projects—showed Cissie around the city and saw to it that she had a good time.

"I was a teenager then, and ever since that event, I always wanted to live in San Diego for some part of my life, even if it was for just a couple of years," Cissie said. "I was always hoping that Corey would get traded or picked up by the San Diego Chargers someday, and when that happened, it showed that even in the little things, the Lord cares."

The couple rented a modest bungalow in the coastal community of Del Mar, where they loved taking beach walks with their dog. On the playing field, Corey had a strong season with the Chargers in 2012, playing in all sixteen games and taking over a starting role for the last six games of the season in an injury-depleted secondary. He recovered a couple of fumbles on special teams, and his second-half interception against the New York Jets thwarted a rally and preserved a win. The Chargers, however, lost too many close games and finished with a 7–9 record, costing head coach Norv Turner his job.

Corey will have to impress a new coaching staff in 2013, but he's used to the drill. He's also had to get used to learning a new skill—changing diapers. He and Cissie became parents during the first month of the 2013 NFL season.

HIS SOURCE OF SUPPORT

Never in her wildest dreams did Cissie Graham Lynch ever expect to be married to a professional football player. Now, she jokingly calls herself an "NFL wife." But she would tell anyone that the NFL lifestyle is not as glamorous as it looks from the outside.

Being married to an NFL player means sharing the pressures and stress that come from being part of an industry in which a husband's career could end any day—either on the field due to a debilitating injury or through a coaching staff decision to "go in a different direction"—the phrase coaches always use when they cut a player.

You learn to travel light when your husband plays in the NFL. When the Buccaneers called Corey to tell him they were picking him up from the Bengals practice squad, he and Cissie packed up their stuff that night and drove to Tampa Bay the following morning. "We haven't been back to Cincinnati since," Cissie said.

"You have to be quite flexible, but I enjoy it," she added. "I know the NFL is a short time in our lives. Everything has been an adventure, and it's been fun getting to know new cities and trying them out."

Corey and Cissie have found their couples' Bible studies a great source of support. "I couldn't think what our experience would be like without those Bible studies," she said. "That's where we've formed some of our greatest friendships and gotten to know the guys outside of football in a stress-free environment where people can be themselves."

Things were a bit different in San Diego, where there wasn't a couples' study during the 2012 season, though four or five players' wives and a coach's wife gathered together on Wednesday nights. Cissie and Corey noticed, however, that they were called upon to minister to others in the Chargers family. Corey often received phone calls from players dealing with issues in their lives, and he'd drop everything to go talk to them. Cissie bonded with some players' wives and was a listening ear.

"We know without a shadow of doubt that is where the Lord has placed us," Cissie said. "This is our mission field. I've seen how the NFL has given Corey opportunities to share the gospel and be an example of a godly man."

The NFL has also given Corey opportunities to be . . . mocked. Teased about his faith. Singled out. Sometimes teammates would hold up a smartphone with an inappropriate image on the screen.

Take a look, Corey.

He would turn his face away. Then there are the little digs, the snide comments. Players knew they were wasting their breath inviting him to nightclubs like Stingaree in the Gaslamp Quarter.

"Wherever you are in life, when you take a stand for the Lord, it's not going to be easy," Cissie said.

If the NFL is a mission field—and it is—then it's one of the hardest mission fields out there. This is due to the instant respect that being an NFL player commands in social situations, the money, and how players have been told they are something special since they were fifteen years old—or younger. Corey and Cissie understand that being in the NFL has given each of them a platform to share the Good News of Jesus Christ.

"I thank the Lord for the opportunity," she said, "and I'm overwhelmed by God's goodness toward Corey and myself, giving us this platform in the NFL. There's no question that we see God's hand in all of this. I'm grateful for where we are, even with the negatives that come with pro football because I look at this as being for such a short time. Our identity is in something greater than the NFL, so the craziness and the lifestyle don't stress us out."

It's possible that when Corey's career comes to an end, he and Cissie could move to a different mission field—perhaps giving legs and feet to the gospel through Samaritan's Purse. Cissie has worked as a special projects producer with the Billy Graham Evangelistic Association (BGEA) as well as with her father's ministry, which includes being the on-camera talent for a series of videos representing these organizations.

I watched a few of the videos and thought she did a great job when she led a camera crew to the corner of Washington and Hill streets in downtown Los Angeles. I marveled that this was the site of the "Canvas Cathedral"—where her grandfather first got national attention when he preached under a tent for eight consecutive weeks in 1949.

Then a film crew followed her to Hollywood Boulevard, where she found Billy Graham's star on the Walk of Fame. "He was just a preacher from North Carolina who has honored and obeyed the Lord," she said to the camera.

And now the third generation of Grahams—and maybe a Lynch—is poised to carry the torch.

2

JOHNATHAN FRANKLIN: SEVENTH ON THE DEPTH CHART

When Johnathan Franklin was playing football at UCLA, he did his banking at the University Credit Union branch along Bruin Walk, the main promenade through the bucolic campus in Los Angeles' Westside. There was an older guy he'd occasionally run into at the ATM. He wore khaki trousers and a white polo shirt that identified him as part of the UCLA custodial staff.

"Hey, wassup, Frankie?" he'd say in a shoot-the-breeze manner.

Johnathan was used to recognition on the UCLA campus. He was a Bruin football player, after all, the starting running back for two seasons. Having students, alums, and boosters recognize him came with the territory. But this fellow was different. Nobody had ever made a nickname out of his last name.

Johnathan smiled. "Nuttin' much," he replied. "How are you?"

The UCLA janitor drew closer. "I'm fine, but how's everything with you, man? We should link up some time."

Johnathan sized up the custodian. They were both African-Americans on a campus where the student body of 40,000 was predominantly Asian-American (37 percent) and white (31 percent). He was a brother, and something about his friendly request to meet up sometime piqued Johnathan's curiosity.

"Take my number," Johnathan said, then dictated his cell number. Like most college students in Westwood, Johnathan managed his life and his contacts through his iPhone.

A week later, Keenan Riggs, the janitor, sent a simple text: Let's link up.

It was the off-season, May 2011, so Johnathan had the time. He had recently finished the spring practices heading into his junior season.

Johnathan and Keenan met at the steps to Ackerman Union, the midpoint of Bruin Walk. Keenan didn't waste time getting to why he wanted to meet with Johnathan. He immediately began talking about God and what it meant to have a personal relationship with His Son, Jesus Christ.

Johnathan listened. He had gone to church as a little kid and knew about God. He knew his mother was one of those "praying moms." He believed that Jesus died on a cross for him, although in his heart of hearts he wasn't sure if he really knew who Jesus was. Johnathan was too busy being a football player and a student to think about that. The pretty girls who flocked in his direction were a distraction, too.

Johnathan had come into his own with a big sophomore season the previous fall. He had led the Bruins in rushing with 1,127 yards, the tenth-best mark in school history. He showed an ability to explode out of his cuts and weave through traffic. His coaches were saying that if he kept working hard, he could break a lot of UCLA records.

Johnathan was enjoying the conversation with Keenan, who was married with two children at home. He could tell he was a salt-of-the-earth kind of guy, someone who put in an honest day's work cleaning classrooms and mopping hallways. He was interested in what Keenan had to say. Truth be known, even though he was a football star at a high-profile school, Johnathan felt something was missing in his life. He was hungry for something more than being known as one of the best running backs in the Pac-12 Conference.

Keenan tapped him on the knee. "I know you have the Holy Spirit in you because you're understanding what I'm saying," the janitor said. "If you didn't have the Holy Spirit in you, you'd be looking at me like I'm stupid."

You've got a point there, Johnathan thought.

The two men agreed to continue the discussion the next day. Their dialogue centered around what it meant to follow Jesus and the promise of eternal life. Hearing Keenan talk was like adding another layer of bricks to Johnathan's spiritual foundation.

"Come to the King's Table on Saturday night," Keenan said before they parted.

At first, Johnathan didn't know what the King's Table was all about, but he soon found out that it was a men's Bible study. When Johnathan arrived at the home of the person hosting the evening, he was welcomed as just another guy. After settling in, they listened to a speaker issue a challenge to everyone in the room.

"How many of you are looking for worldly things to satisfy you?" he asked. "How many of you guys drink to satisfy yourself? Do drugs to satisfy yourself? Go to parties to find women to satisfy yourself?"

Johnathan dropped his head. At one time or another, he had done all those things—not so much the drugs part, but the drinking and being with the ladies.

"How many of those things in this world really satisfy you?" the speaker asked. "Or do you just want more and more and more?"

He was right. With everything Johnathan had accomplished as a football player, he still wanted more—more touchdowns, more cheers, more glory, more media attention. He was never content with his situation, no matter how well he ran on the Rose Bowl's natural turf.

"The only thing that can satisfy you is Jesus Christ," the speaker continued. "Let Him come into your life. Let Him give you peace. Let Him give you true satisfaction. Come, receive Him into your heart."

Johnathan had heard preaching like that growing up in Baldwin Hills, a suburb a few miles south of downtown Los Angeles. This time, though, he had a feeling he'd never felt before. A peace settled over him—a peace he couldn't understand. That evening, he gave his life to Christ.

"I was like wow, I can't describe it," Johnathan said. "The speaker reminded me that accepting Jesus wouldn't mean that everything was going to be goodie-goodie from now on.

He said I would still have my bumps and bruises, but accepting Him would mean knowing I had someone with me every step of the way. Knowing that I would have peace. Knowing that I would have joy. Knowing that I could be used. Knowing that I'd finally be satisfied. That night, my life totally changed."

GOD WORKS IN MYSTERIOUS WAYS

For the past few years, I've attended the Holiday Bowl prayer breakfast in San Diego. The cause is a good one—to support the Christian players on both teams as well as the San Diego chapter of the Fellowship of Christian Athletes. The annual event draws 800 or so people to a downtown ballroom.

The breakfast is held the morning of the game, so it isn't easy to get players from either team to show up. Every year, around a dozen or so players would be there, although I remember one year when University of Texas head coach Mack Brown escorted the *entire* Longhorn team to the breakfast. Coach Brown had made the prayer breakfast a mandatory game day team event.

That morning, Miles McPherson, a former Chargers player and pastor of The Rock, a megachurch of 12,000 near Lindbergh Field, delivered one of his patented evangelistic messages. When it came time for the "altar call," about a dozen Longhorn players stood up to acknowledge their decision to follow Christ.

The 2012 Holiday Bowl matched UCLA against Baylor University. Johnathan Franklin, the senior running back playing in his final collegiate game, was asked to come to the stage, where one of the local FCA leaders interviewed him. When asked how he came to the Lord, Johnathan said a UCLA janitor was responsible, but he didn't elaborate.

Now that sounded interesting. When Johnathan finished his presentation, I approached him and asked him about being part of this book, which was yet another example of how God really orchestrates our steps.

THE EARLY YEARS

Baldwin Hills, the Los Angeles suburb where Johnathan grew up, is known as the "black Beverly Hills" for two reasons: it's predominantly African-American and it's one of the wealthiest majority-black areas in the United States.

Located a few miles south of downtown, Baldwin Hills isn't filled with gated mansions like its storied neighbor to the north but is home to the largest middle and upper-middle-class black community in Southern California. Johnathan, however, grew up in "lower" Baldwin Hills, in a less affluent neighborhood known as "The Jungle," where drug dealing and flying bullets were part of life.

"We lived in the rough part of Baldwin Hills," Johnathan said. "Pretty much everybody was in gangs. I know a lot of guys who are in jail or going to jail. I saw a lot of shootings. I could probably name ten people I know who've been shot. That number has been growing since I graduated from high school. Thankfully, I had a mother who kept me strong."

Johnathan's mother, a single parent, did her best to protect him and his older sister from the streets. One way she did that was to get Johnathan involved in sports, especially football. He was a standout at Dorsey High, where he played linebacker and running back. He was known as "Jet Ski," a nickname he got in fifth grade when he was racing a teammate on his Pop

Warner football team after practice. "Back then, we had a dirt field, so when I was racing him, dust was coming up behind my feet like water does behind a jet ski," Johnathan explained. By the time he reached high school, "Jet Ski" was known for his smooth, explosive speed, which left defenses in his wake.

He also had another nickname—"Hollywood." During his senior year at Dorsey High, he was one of the "cast members" on the reality show, *Baldwin Hills*, which aired on the BET (Black Entertainment Television) cable network. *Baldwin Hills*, which ran for three seasons, was the African-American version of MTV's *Laguna Beach: The Real Orange County*. The show followed the lives of nine or ten Dorsey High students, focusing on storylines about their teen angst—the drama surrounding who's dating who and what dress to wear on Saturday nights.

Johnathan was a thoughtful, all-around student in high school. Sometimes he'd sit outside and write about what he saw around him. He followed his muse by penning poetry, but not the kind of lovey-dovey couplets that girls swoon over. He wrote about people bettering themselves or making a difference in their community. One time, he shared those thoughts at open-mic night at Da Poetry Lounge in Hollywood. On another occasion, he took a crack at writing a book for teens about the influence of music, about why guys wear pants that sag, and how the "N-word" and "B-word" are both derogatory and demeaning.

Johnathan became interested in the student council and ran for class president his senior year. When the votes were counted, he and a girl were tied for first place. Johnathan missed giving a speech for the runoff because he was in Northern California for a state track meet, so the young woman he had run against was awarded the class presidency.

UCLA recruited Johnathan as an "athlete," meaning the Bruin coaches would find a position that matched his talent after he arrived on campus. At 5 feet, 11 inches and 180 pounds, he wasn't quite linebacker material, and the team was stockpiled at running back. At the start of his freshman year at Westwood, the Bruins coaching staff told him they would be redshirting him and prepping him to play safety.

That development didn't sit well with Johnathan. He had never played that position before, so he told his coaches he wanted to be a running back.

Okay, but you'll have to get in line, son. You're seventh on the depth chart.

When you're at the bottom of the depth chart, you're practically a forgotten man. Coaches barely talked to Johnathan, and teammates didn't even acknowledge his existence. He might as well have been shipped to the University of Siberia.

The cold shoulders weren't going to stop him, though. Exiled to the scout team (scout teams are made up of redshirting freshman and other players who scrimmage against the starting teams to prep them for upcoming games) during his redshirt year, he attacked the UCLA first-team defense like it was fourth quarter of the big rivalry game against USC. When the season was over, Johnathan was named co-winner of the Charles Pike Memorial Award for his outstanding scout team play.

Johnathan kept working hard, and during spring ball prior to the 2009 season, he leapfrogged over his competition. He emerged from summer training camp as the Bruins' starting running back. Coaches loved his quickness out of the gate. His loose hips and quick feet gave him the ability to cut inside the defensive back and into open space. That is, when the ball wasn't being popped loose from his grip.

Johnathan fumbled seven times during his redshirt freshman season, losing three. After eight games as a starter, he was firmly entrenched in head coach Rick Neuheisel's doghouse. He didn't play much the rest of the season for a team that finished 7–6 after a bowl win over Temple.

Give him credit: Johnathan addressed his fumblitis head-on. He decided to carry a football around campus during the off-season—to classes, to the weight room, and back to his dorm. Whenever he saw his teammates, he dared them to try to strip the ball from his arms. They were never successful, which helped Johnathan get over the mental hurdle of thinking he was a fumbler. He also bulked up to 200 pounds and gained strength gripping the ball.

No doubt enamored with the moves he showed off in practice, Coach Neuheisel gave Johnathan another chance. He responded with some excellent games on his way to rushing for more than 1,000 yards his sophomore year. But in the cross-town game against USC, Johnathan got popped and lost the ball again. A Trojan linebacker scooped up the loose football and sprinted 68 yards for a touchdown, which contributed heavily to a 25–14 UCLA loss. Bruin fans torched "Fumble Franklin" in the blogosphere.

No way Johnathan would give up, though.

Keep in mind that all this was swirling around when Keenan Riggs, the UCLA janitor, reached out to Johnathan in the spring of 2011, which led him to accept Christ into his heart at the King's Table.

"When I surrendered to God, I said, 'Lord, I don't care what my teammates say. I don't care what the girls say. I don't care if people judge me, but I'm going to live for You,' " he explained. This wasn't a halfhearted acceptance of Christ into his life. He was sold out for the Lord.

Johnathan extended his teammates an open invitation to attend a Bible study. He led the team in prayer after practice. He cracked open his Bible while dressing before games and read Scripture verses out loud to anyone who wanted to listen. He became a quiet leader on the team and was careful which groups he socialized with away from the football field.

When Johnathan became a Christian, he was acutely aware that life wouldn't be sunny the rest of the way or that he'd never fumble again. His junior season, he said, was average, but he still led the team with 976 yards rushing and averaged a career-best 5.9 yards per carry.

His senior season in 2012 was when Johnathan went from being a very good college running back to being someone who can run for daylight on Sundays. He kicked off the season with 200-yard games against Rice and Nebraska on the way to establishing new single-season school records for rushing yards and all-purpose yards. Johnathan's long touchdown runs were a catalyst to UCLA's best season in years. The Bruins finished with a 9–5 record, including a close loss to Stanford in the Pac-12 Championship Game. And he cleaned up his fumbling issues.

Johnathan's fast finish to his college career prompted a fourth-round selection by the Green Bay Packers, who also grabbed another running back, Alabama's Eddie Lacy, in round two. After going 43 consecutive games without a running back hitting 100 yards, the Packers wanted to shake up a stale backfield. The pair of rookies will likely do that.

Mission accomplished, reaching the NFL, but Johnathan is sure that professional football won't be the end all of why God has him on this earth. He sees football as an important stepping stone to a career in . . . politics.

SAY A QUICK PRAYER

Johnathan Franklin has a ritual before every play.

While taking his spot in the backfield, he says, "Father, Son, Holy Spirit," and then he whispers to himself, *God, run with me. God, catch with me. God, score with me.*

FRANKLIN FOR MAYOR

When Johnathan was in elementary school, one of his teachers gave him an assignment: read something on current events.

He groaned, as most high-spirited boys do at that age when their teacher gives them that kind of assignment. This meant reading the front page of the *Los Angeles Times*, or perhaps an article in the local section. His teacher's reading assignment wasn't as fun as playing video games.

But a seed was planted in Johnathan when he read the newspaper. He learned that there was another world out there—a world of grown-ups making decisions about how we live, settle our differences, and build for the future.

Flash forward to his senior year at Dorsey High. Every morning at 6:30, Johnathan was among a group of football players who showed up in a cramped, roach-infested weight room to get some work done before class. Leading them was a volunteer coach, Martin Ludlow, who knew a lot about City Hall but not that much about the X's and O's of football.

Ludlow was there because he wanted to give back to the community. He was a political operative with experience at L.A. City Hall and with the state government in Sacramento. He had worked behind the scenes where the levers of power were pushed. He'd been a close aide to Antonio Villaraigosa when the future Los Angeles mayor was in the California State Assembly. In 2003, Ludlow branched out on his own and was elected to the L.A. City Council.

Ludlow took an interest in Johnathan and became a male role model for him. In Johnathan, Ludow saw something more than a football player. Perhaps it was Johnathan's willing-to-learn demeanor or the earnest way he asked questions about what it was like to be on the L.A. City Council. A bond formed between the two as they discussed man-to-man the issues facing the community.

The dialogues fired Johnathan's imagination. One morning after weight lifting, Johnathan confided to Coach Ludlow that he wanted to do something big with his life, that he wanted to make an impact off the field. "I think I want to get into politics," he said. "Someday, I would like to become the mayor of Los Angeles."

Coach Ludlow nodded. He wasn't about to squash those dreams. He encouraged Johnathan to continue thinking that way. When Johnathan went off to UCLA, he majored in political science with an eye toward future public service. During the spring of 2011, he talked to Ludlow about getting a one-week internship at City Hall. Ludlow and Mayor

Villaraigosa had a long relationship, so doors swung open for the UCLA football player.

On the first day of his internship, Johnathan shadowed the mayor like a spy linebacker who kept his eyes on a dual-threat quarterback. He also got to sit down in the mayor's paneled office and ask questions about how things got done in city government.

The following day, he tagged along with Los Angeles Police Chief Charles Beck as he made his rounds. That included a helicopter ride above the busy metropolis and its tangle of congested freeways. He received a tutorial about the "thin, blue line" between good, upstanding citizens and those who perpetrate crimes against the populace.

Johnathan spent another day sitting in on meetings between representatives from various chambers of commerce. "We were in a big courtroom with thirty or forty people," Johnathan said. "Each person had five or ten minutes to talk about the problems they were facing in their communities. I sat in the back and said to myself, *Los Angeles needs somebody to make changes. There are so many voices out there that are unheard. There are some voices out there that are not acknowledged. I want to be able to do what's best for everyone.*

"If I ever get a chance, I want to make changes in L.A. There are too many things that are overlooked. But hearing all those voices say that they need this and they need that really opened my eyes to understanding that life is more than football, and that it's not just about me or my struggles. It's *our* struggles. My internship really got me going and has motivated me to try to become mayor someday."

Hearing Johnathan say that prompted this conversation between us:

What are two or three things that you'd really like to work on for the city?

Johnathan: The first is education, which is unfair. I grew up in the inner city. I went to Dorsey High School. I'm going to compare my school to Beverly Hills High School. If you take a kid from the inner city, from a rough neighborhood, and he has a 3.5 grade-point average, and then you compare that kid to a kid from Beverley Hills with a 3.5, the kid in Beverly Hills will have an advantage just because of the school and the neighborhood he grew up in.

There are many kids from the inner city who get overlooked, aren't acknowledged, and don't have the opportunity to go to college. Potential employers will look at their applications and throw them out just because of where they come from or the school they attended. It shouldn't be like that.

So many kids who end up doing what they shouldn't be doing are not becoming anything in life because they don't have the same opportunity as other people in other neighborhoods. I want to see things change so that regardless of what school you went to, regardless of where you came from, you can become something. You can go to college, you can become a doctor. Your school should not prevent you from going to college, but in the inner city, at high schools like Dorsey, Crenshaw, Manual Arts, or Jefferson, that's how it's been.

Does that mean that those schools need to get better?

Johnathan: Definitely.

How does a school get better?

Johnathan: More discipline. More testing. Better preparation of students for life after school. Having speakers coming in to motivate them. In the inner city, the stereotype is that the kids are never going to amount to anything. That needs to change. Everyone should be pushed in the inner city to be great. The education system should be fair. Fifty-one percent of the kids in the inner city don't make it to college.

What's another thing you couldn't wait to work on if you were mayor?

Johnathan: I don't know how we'd do it, but we're overpopulated with homelessness. I understand that people make mistakes. Some people have to help themselves. When I've gone down to Skid Row, it's hurt me to see all the homeless people. We're talking about thousands on the streets. We need to do something about that, even if that means building more shelters.

Skid Row is so bad. The dirtiness of it reeks. It needs to be cleaned up. I would definitely want to tackle this homeless problem. I don't know exactly how, but I know it can be done. There's not a problem in L.A. that can't be solved, but we need to deal with it. I'm just hoping I get the chance to be part of the solution.

When word got around that Johnathan would like to be mayor of Los Angeles when he's done playing football, some enterprising UCLA students silkscreened "The Mayor" above a large 23 (his number at UCLA) and "J. Franklin 2012" below. The T-shirts were handed out in the student section.

That's a nice idea, but I think they got the year wrong. I'm thinking the mayor's race in 2025 could be a doozy. By then, Johnathan's NFL career will be in the past and he will be thirty-six years old, certainly old enough and mature enough for Los Angeles voters to entrust him with the mayor's office.

ANOTHER PATH TO SERVING

If politics doesn't work out, maybe evangelism is in Johnathan's future. He has that infectious quality that draws people to him, and it helps that he's the quiet leader type.

Going into his senior season at UCLA, Johnathan felt his heart stirring over how many people needed to hear about God. He started his outreach by approaching redshirt freshman quarterback Brett Hundley, who won the starting job in training camp. He invited Hundley to drop by his apartment, where they'd pop open the Bible and study and pray together. Word of their prayer times got around the locker room, and by the middle of the season, more than twenty UCLA football players were regularly meeting to study and discuss God's Word.

The UCLA coaching staff practically made Johnathan the team chaplain. They asked him to pray before Friday night team dinners, pray before the pregame meals on Saturday, pray before the game, and pray *after* the game. "And every day after practice, about thirty-five guys would get together and pray," Johnathan said. "Seeing young men wanting to know Christ was such a blessing.

"I saw so many guys on my team find Christ because of God using me. It was humbling to see how God works and how God moves."

UCLA had a turnaround season on and off the field in 2012. There was the 9–5 record on the field, but off the field, what really made an impression on Johnathan was when students would stop him on campus and say, "Thank you for being a light. You encourage me."

If there's something Johnathan learned that year, it's how God can use him in mighty ways. "I feel like God's placing me on a platform to be used. I don't know why, but it's happened," he said.

"I remember someone telling me, 'God uses us like a mom.' When you're a little kid, your mom wouldn't want you to leave the house looking crazy. She wants you looking good because you're representing her. After you've accepted Him, He's going to send you out in the world to represent Him and be a light. Yes, I've done successful things, but it's not for my glory but for God's glory, to represent Him.

"God has blessed me so much this past year and placed me on so many great platforms to talk to people and be in front of great people and be a witness in many ways. It's been such a blessing and so humbling. I've come from a guy who was seventh on the depth chart, who always fumbled, and now I'm going into the NFL. I've seen what faith and perseverance can do. God has put me on such a platform and shown me so much favor. I just want to tell the world."

He'll get a chance to do that in Green Bay, one of the

higher-profile NFL franchises. He's already had some practice, though. Before the 2013 NFL draft, Johnathan accepted an invitation to share his testimony at an event that meant a great deal to him—the fortieth annual Mayor's Prayer Breakfast.

Los Angeles Mayor Antonio Villaraigosa listened from the dais, and Johnathan couldn't help but wonder if he'll ever sit in that seat.

There's one thing about politics that's clearly in Johnathan's favor: he knows how to run.

HE SAID IT

"I'm a man of God, and I'm a role model in my community. I never want to be remembered as just Johnathan Franklin, the running back who rushed for 1,000 yards. My life won't be complete until I impact other lives."

—Johnathan Franklin, who considers football to be only 30 percent of who he is as a person

3

ANDY STUDEBAKER:
HANDS OFF THE WHEEL

Here's a scene from the popular TV game show *Jeopardy* that I'd like to see in the future:

Harvard professor dressed in tweed jacket with elbow patches: "I'll take NFL Players for $800, Alex."

Alex Trebek, the erudite, longtime host of *Jeopardy*: "This former Division III player is named after a car company."

(Quick buzzing sound) **Nerdy beanpole with thick-rimmed black glasses:** "Who is Cameron Ford?"

Alex Trebek: "Wrong. Cameron Ford, a tight end with the Green Bay Packers, played for Wake Forest, a Division I school."

(Quick buzzing sound) **Attractive female attorney in her mid-thirties:** "Who is Justin Tucker?"

Alex Trebek: "Wrong again. Yes, there was a Tucker car

in the late 1940s, and Justin Tucker is a kicker for the Baltimore Ravens, but he played for the University of Texas."

Trebek looks toward the Harvard professor, who shrugs his shoulders and then presses the buzzer anyway. "Who is Mercury Morris?" he says unconvincingly.

Alex Trebek: "Good stab, but we're looking for *last names*. Besides, 'Mercury' was Eugene Edward Morris' nickname, and he played at West Texas State."

At this point, I'm beside myself because I know the answer. (Doesn't everyone when they're watching *Jeopardy*?) I'm yelling at the television: *Who is Andy Studebaker? Who is Andy Studebaker?*

The time beeper sounds, and Alex Trebek reveals that I had it right: Andy Studebaker, a Kansas City Chiefs outside linebacker, played at Wheaton College, a Division III school near Chicago.

Andy is also the great-great-great-great-great-great grandson—that's nine generations—of Peter Studebaker, an eighteenth-century Midwestern blacksmith who turned a thriving wagon and carriage business into a family-run enterprise that would eventually produce millions of cars, trucks, and buses under the Studebaker nameplate during the first half of the twentieth century.

But that's in Andy's family background—and it didn't do anything to pave a smooth highway to the League. Here's the deal: If the odds are exceedingly low for someone from an FCS school (Division I-AA), like Corey Lynch, to make it to the NFL, they are positively off the charts for someone who played football at a Division III school.

You see, during the 2012 season, you could comfortably

seat every former Division III player in the NFL inside a 1950s-vintage Studebaker bullet-nose sedan:

• **Pierre Garçon,** the Washington Redskins wide receiver who is of Haitian descent, played at the University of Mount Union in Alliance, Ohio. He was Robert Griffin III's favorite target during the 'Skins' 2012 run to the NFL playoffs.

• **Cecil Shorts III,** a wide receiver for the Jacksonville Jaguars, also played at Mount Union. (Who's their receivers coach?)

• **London Fletcher,** a middle linebacker for the Washington Redskins, has put together a distinguished fifteen-year career in the NFL after being undrafted out of John Carroll University, a Jesuit institution in University Heights, Ohio. He is the heart and soul of the Redskins defense as well as its captain and leader.

• **Andy Studebaker,** who's played five seasons with the Kansas City Chiefs, graduated from a college that's better known for being evangelist Billy Graham's alma mater than for its football team.

As Andy said, "It's the hand of the Lord."

THE HISTORY OF STUDEBAKER

Most young people have likely never heard of Studebaker cars, which had a good run from the early 1900s until being sidetracked by the Great Depression in the 1930s, then hitting smooth road in the 1950s before being dusted by the competition and shutting down in the 1960s. The last Studebaker rolled out of the factory in 1966.

Andy's father, Ken, knew what it was like to ride in a car with your name on it. His father owned a Champion, whose distinctive bullet-nose cone made it the most recognizable Studebaker ever made.

ALWAYS IN GEAR

As the fifth and final child to come off Ken and Jane Studebaker's assembly line, Andy grew up in a long line of Studebakers. Five children were born in a span of six years, which meant Ken and Jane were up to their armpits in diapers for nearly a decade. In terms of models, Ben hit the showroom floor first, followed by Becky, Rachel, Daniel, and Andrew, as his parents still call him today.

When you're fifth on the family depth chart, you can count on two things growing up:

1. Your older brothers and sisters will blame you for anything that goes wrong.

2. You'll have to speak up for yourself—or be willing to fight for something you want.

Take a simple task like eating breakfast cereal in the morning. Picture the scene: Andy, four years old, is sitting at the dining room table with his four older brothers and sisters. The lazy Susan spins with boxes of Lucky Charms, Captain Crunch, Fruity Pebbles, and Peanut Butter Captain Crunch. The older children grab boxes right and left and pour heaping helpings into their bowls—while Andy grasps at air. He throws elbows and persists until he can clutch a box and fill his bowl with his favorite cereal, Fruity Pebbles.

"Andrew might have been the last one to get cereal, but he always held his own," Jane said. "Even back then, he was a fighter. He did not stand back and let his brothers and sisters run over him. He was a sturdy little boy who held up his end.

I would call him a survivor more than anything else."

Ken says Andy learned to stand up for himself because his siblings were always yelling, "He did it, Dad!"

"Now that the kids are older and having children of their own, they are admitting the truth, which is that Andy got into a lot of trouble that he shouldn't have," Ken said. "With five kids, there was always something going on all the time, and Andy was the one catching the flak."

The Studebaker family lived amid the checkerboard farmlands of central Illinois in a blink-and-miss-it town called Congerville, population 474. The thousands who drive by the town's outskirts on Interstate 74 barely notice the sleepy hamlet located eighteen freeway miles northwest of Bloomington and twenty-three miles east of Peoria.

The joke in Congerville is that Jane's family—the Steffens—accounted for half the town's population. On Ken and Jane's street, Jane's brother Kent, his wife Beth, and their four children lived next door to the west. Jane's parents lived one hundred yards to the east. Ken's parents, Paul and Shirley Studebaker, lived in Eureka.

"All of Jane's family, except for a brother who now lives in Florida, lived in the neighborhood or within four or five miles of us," Ken said. "Besides my parents, Andy also grew up around his cousins and aunts and uncles on my side because there are plenty of Studebakers in Indiana. Between my wife and me, there was always family around him."

In and around Congerville, there were eleven cousins for Andy and his older brothers and sisters to play with. The kids were always messing around in each other's backyards, playing tackle football (without pads) or knocking around a baseball in open fields. The other big activity was hockey. They played roller hockey in the driveway until the annual cold snap in December and January froze a nearby pond, which meant the kids could put on ice skates and play "real" hockey.

Andy wasn't a hyperactive kid growing up (in any ADHD sort of way), but he always seemed to be revved up. Watching TV was too slow for him; he often lay on the floor and tossed the remote up in the air and caught it—most of the time. He had trouble falling asleep at night because he had wound himself up so high during the day, like a tachometer pushing the redline.

The Studebakers drove a lot to nearby Eureka, population 5,000, where the kids went to school and the family went to church. Andy had to learn to sit still in church, but it wasn't easy dialing down the RPMs. The family attended Eureka Bible Church, a small congregation that's part of the Fellowship of Evangelical Churches conference. "I grew up in the church," Andy said. "I've been a Christian as long as I can remember. As much as it would be nice to have a 'road to Damascus' experience, I don't recall a certain time when my life was completely altered."

Life in the Studebaker home revolved around church, school, sports, and family. Or maybe sports, family, church, and school. Wherever sports ranked in the Studebaker household, all five children were "in season" year round. At Eureka High School, Ben was a three-sport athlete: golf, basketball, and baseball. Becky lettered in track and cross country. Rachel was a volleyball player who also played softball. Daniel was a three-sport athlete: football, wrestling, and baseball.

Andy played three sports as well: football, basketball, and track, where he was a high jumper and relay runner.

BEN ZOBRIST, EUREKA!

If you've read some of my other books, like *Playing with Purpose: Inside the Lives and Faith of the Major Leagues' Top Players*, you might recognize the town of Eureka, Illinois, which is the home of Eureka College, the alma mater of President Ronald Reagan, who graduated in 1932.

Eureka is also the hometown of Ben Zobrist, the Tampa Bay Rays ballplayer who has quietly put together a solid major league career. Tom and Cindi Zobrist have also raised five children, and several of them were middle school and high school classmates of the five Studebaker children in Eureka. Jessica Zobrist, Ben's oldest sister, and Ben Studebaker, Andy's oldest brother, were best friends in high school. (Anyone getting confused?) Also, Ben Z. played baseball with Ben S. at Eureka High.

Ben Zobrist, like Andy, has an incredible story of how he overcame insurmountable odds to play a professional sport. Ben is playing in the major leagues today because he agreed to pay $50 of his own money for a college baseball tryout two weeks after he graduated from high school. The coach at Olivet Nazarene witnessed the tryout, offered him a scholarship, and Ben—who was planning to attend Calvary Bible College in Kansas City (ironic, given that's where Andy Studebaker lives today)—said yes.

You'll have to read the baseball edition of *Playing with Purpose* to find out the rest of the story, but it's an amazing account of how the small town of Eureka, Illinois, sent two of its favorite sons to Major League Baseball and the National Football League.

Ken and Jane let their children know early on that they weren't going to be the type of parents who'd intervene with coaches regarding playing time or what position they should play. "We told the kids, 'Don't expect to be a starter right away. You have to get your cards punched. Play your part,' " Ken said. "We certainly talked to all of our children, including Andrew, about the virtue of patience."

Ken, a technical business analyst for State Farm Insurance, and Jane, a registered nurse who worked the graveyard shift at Peoria's St. Francis Medical Center so that she could be with the kids during the day, loved those kinds of teachable moments. They were also volunteer teachers at Eureka Bible Church, where Ken taught the high school youth group while Jane tended to preschoolers. When the children hit their high school years, they sat among peers while Dad led conversations about dating, drinking, and other hot-button issues.

"It helped me to have all five kids come through," Ken said. "They didn't sit like lumps on a log. They were involved in the conversations and in the lessons."

During Andy's teen years, Dad noticed something about his youngest son: he was the most driven and ambitious of his five children. Andy put his drive on display during the summer vacations the family took at Table Rock Lake, near Branson, Missouri. One time, when the family went boating on the lake, they parked at an island to eat a picnic lunch. While Jane was cooking hot dogs, Ken picked up a flat rock about six inches thick and two feet wide and weighing around thirty pounds and tossed it into eight or nine feet of water.

"Hey, Andy! Fetch!" he jokingly said.

Andy sprinted to the water's edge and dove in. He swam

to the spot where his father had thrown the rock, dove to the bottom of the deep, blue water, and returned to the surface ten seconds later carrying the rock over his head. "I bet we did this fifteen times," Ken said. "Andy showed no fear. None of my other kids would have done that."

When Andy was in high school, his determination to keep pushing himself showed itself in the weight room, where he shaped his body into a muscular 6-foot, 3-inch, 215-pound specimen. On the football field, Andy dominated the line of scrimmage as a tight end and defensive end.

Despite being one of the best players in his region, Andy elicited no interest from Division I colleges. Playing for a small high school with just 500 students hurt his chances to play college football at the highest level.

Andy's brother Daniel, who was a grade ahead of him, was a freshman at Wheaton College who'd tried out for and made the football team. Since Eureka was only two hours from the Wheaton campus, Andy attended several of Daniel's home games during the fall of his senior year in high school. He became acquainted with the football coaches, who took an interest in having another Studebaker roll into Wheaton, a Division III school. Wheaton didn't offer athletic scholarships but had a serious football program that was a perennial powerhouse in the College Conference of Illinois and Wisconsin (CCIW), playing schools such as Elmhurst, Augustana, and Illinois Wesleyan.

Since Wheaton showed the most interest (other CCIW schools recruited him as well), the die was cast. Playing alongside his brother on a college football field would be awesome, Andy thought. So would be attending Wheaton

College, the "evangelical Harvard" of Christian higher education. The Wheaton alumni list read like a Who's Who of Christendom:

- Billy Graham, class of '43, the greatest evangelist of the twentieth century
- Jim Elliot, a martyred missionary, and his widow, Elisabeth Elliot
- Ken Taylor, the man behind the *New Living Bible* and founder of Tyndale House Publishers, a Christian publishing company based in nearby Carol Stream
- Philip Yancey, author of books like *What's So Amazing About Grace?*
- Todd Beamer, the hero of United Flight 93 whose phrase, "Let's roll," came to symbolize the ethos of 9/11

One could pick a lot worse place to earn a college degree. Wheaton had an undergraduate enrollment of 2,400 students, who were required to live on campus, either in dorms or apartments. But the campus, tucked away in a bucolic setting and dotted with ivy-covered stone buildings, was so green and beautiful, why would anyone want to leave? Besides, downtown Chicago was a twenty-mile train ride away.

But what really sold Andy on Wheaton was head coach Mike Swider, who'd been in charge of the football team since 1996 and had created a culture of integrity that permeated the program from top to bottom.

"I knew Wheaton was a great school and a cool place to go to, but I wanted to be around men of high character," Andy said. "I also wanted to be around people like Coach Swider, who said at the end of the day, you're going to look at yourself in the mirror, and you'll either like what you see, or you won't. I knew being around Coach Swider and the other coaches would shape the way I made decisions for the next sixty years of my life, or however long it's going to be."

There was a price to that decision, though. Andy's parents told him and his older brothers and sisters that there was no way they could afford to put all five of them through college. That wasn't going to change now that Andy was the last to leave the nest.

"Even though my parents couldn't afford to pay for college, my father explained that it wasn't an option not to go because I had to earn a college degree to function in today's world," Andy said. "That meant I would have to graduate with college loans. It was as simple as that."

Wheaton had a Harvard-sized reputation for academics but was less expensive to attend than an Ivy League school—but not by much. When Andy attended Wheaton—from 2004 to 2008—the cost for tuition, room and board, books, and incidentals ran close to $35,000 a year. Some small grants and a sibling discount took some of the edge off that astronomical amount.

In order to not accumulate too much college debt, Andy worked for an office furniture store in the summers, unloading semi-trucks and assembling the furniture for delivery. But once school started, Andy kept himself busy playing football, attending class, and studying, so he didn't have a spare minute for part-time work. He picked up odd jobs when football season was over, but they were seasonal—Christmas and spring break. His parents didn't leave Andy to fend for himself completely; they helped out when they could, filling his gas tank on weekend trips home, purchasing bags of groceries for the drive back to Wheaton, and slipping him some walking-around money.

Andy would rack up around $75,000 in student loans by the time he graduated—loans he never expected to pay off with an NFL paycheck.

AN UNLIKELY PATH TO THE NFL

So how did Andy Studebaker, a player that high-powered college football programs didn't bother to recruit, who didn't play a down his freshman year at Wheaton, who suffered a season-ending injury in the fifth game of his *senior* season, make it to the NFL and fashion a five-year career (as of this writing) that makes him eligible for an NFL pension?

Would you believe it had a lot to do with a YouTube video?

Well, that's oversimplifying things a bit, but there's plenty of truth in it.

Andy won a roster spot on the Wheaton football team his freshman year, but he stood on the sidelines the entire season, not playing a down. His coaches didn't even put him in during a 50-point blowout win, which had to be disappointing. Andy finally got the chance to get his uniform dirty as a sophomore. He acquitted himself well that year, but his breakout season came during his junior season, in 2006, when he led the nation—the entire NCAA—in sacks with 17½ and in tackles for a loss with 25½.

Putting up those kinds of numbers suddenly had NFL scouts poking their noses into a school whose name they had never typed into their GPS app: Wheaton College. "A scout dropped by, and I ran a 40-yard dash and did pretty well—a 4.50. After that, doors started flying open," Andy said.

Coach Swider would tell any NFL scout he talked to that Andy was a total team guy with a tremendous work ethic—the type of player who'd run through a brick wall for his coaches and his team. While intangibles like work ethic weigh heavily in any scouting report—as well as the probable notation that he was a "choirboy" playing for a Christian college—there were certain physical parameters he had to meet before he could harbor any hope of playing in the NFL:

- Size? At 6 feet, 3 inches and a chiseled 240 pounds, Andy fit the prototypical build for an NFL linebacker.

- Speed? A 4.50 in the 40 spoke volumes. Plus, he showed better-than-expected athleticism.

- A nose for the ball? Well, he *did* lead the nation in sacks and hurries as a true junior. (Wheaton does not redshirt its players.)

- Determination? Game tapes showed how Andy consistently won the hand-to-hand combat battles whenever he rushed the passer. He displayed excellent chase ability and closing speed.

- Competition? That was the big question mark. Among his Division III peers, Andy stood out like a set of red brake lights on a dark night. But D3 schools never got a chance to play against major college programs, so there was no "Michigan" (see Corey Lynch's story) in Andy's past, no clear way to gauge his ability.

And then came the afternoon when football was ripped away from his grasp like a running back stripped of the ball. In an away game at North Central College in Naperville, Illinois, Andy got caught up in a pile and tore a ligament in his right foot—his push-off foot when the ball was snapped.

Andy's parents rushed to Chicago and insisted that their son see the best specialist for this type of injury. Jane said she probably called this specialist's office every hour for days until he finally won an appointment. The diagnosis was grim. In medical terms, Andy had injured his Lisfranc joint, and the specialist said he would have to operate and insert a screw into his foot. Then Andy would have to stay off his right foot for two months.

Andy's mother says she will never forget seeing him in downtown Chicago, sitting on a bench with his hands on his face. "I could see tears hitting the pavement. He was sobbing because he thought he was done. It was probably one of the hardest things I've ever seen one of my kids go through," she said.

Andy, though, said the injury led to a time of deep spiritual refection and reevaluation.

"I thought that was it—I'd never play football again," Andy said. "There's no doubt my faith was shaken, but then again, football had become sort of an idol to me. Football was all I thought about, all I focused on. When I was faced with confronting my idol, that rocked my world. The scouts stopped coming around. I thought I was done for good, but the injury made me rely on Christ to satisfy me. I was reminded of what should be the most important thing in my life."

After Andy underwent the surgical procedure, he had to use a small scooter-like device for several weeks just to get around. With his right foot placed in a plastic boot, he worked on what he could—his upper body and core. He swam three days a week to build up his cardio fitness. But what hurt Andy as much as his foot was missing various college All-Star games where long shots like himself could make an impression with pro scouts.

By February, Andy had regained some mobility and was cleared to start jogging in a straight line—but no cutting. Meanwhile, the NFL Combine in Indianapolis began late that month, and the big Division I schools held their "pro days" during March to showcase graduating players looking to get drafted. In mid-March, Andy finally got medical clearance to run and train without restrictions, but time was not on his side. The NFL draft was scheduled for April 26–27 at Radio City Music Hall in New York City, where ESPN and the NFL Network would devote prime-time coverage to seven rounds of selections.

Andy had hired an agent, Josh Wright, who began thinking *way* outside the box. Josh suggested that Andy do two things: hold his own pro day and invite NFL scouts to attend, and then record his workout for teams that didn't send a scout.

Before Andy's personal pro day, his agent managed to persuade six teams to bring him in for individual workouts. That meant losing twelve days of weight-room training as Andy flew around the country to show NFL coaching staffs what he was capable of. In some hotels, businessmen and families were startled to discover a large, broad-shouldered young man going down into a three-point stance and practicing explosive starts in the hallways.

On April 18, just eight days before the draft, Andy held his pro day at Northwestern University's indoor football training facility—which he had to rent with his own money. The pro day was for him and him only, and seven teams sent scouts to watch.

Holding a digital camera at the training facility was Josh Wright's wife, Carol, an Emmy Award-winning television producer. She trained the camera on Andy as scouts put him through the paces: a 36½-inch vertical leap; a 10-foot, 7-inch standing broad jump; a 4.60 40-yard dash; a 6.81 three-cone dash; an 11.59 60-yard shuttle; and various flexibility drills that showed off his athleticism, footwork, and intensity.

"I was hoping for a shot in the dark," Andy said. "I didn't know what would happen that day, but I had a really good pro day."

Teams asked Wright to overnight a DVD of the footage, but, as many people know, there's a faster way to allow people to watch your video: post it on YouTube. Carol edited the footage, added a little music to the beginning and end, and, within a couple of hours, uploaded the four-minute video—plus a couple of other "highlight reel" clips from Andy's college days—onto YouTube. Josh then emailed links to the YouTube videos to all the NFL teams.

I've watched Andy's pro day on YouTube, and I saw the passion that Andy brought to the field that day. Then again, he was, as they say on *American Idol*, "singing for his life." (I'm also amazed that more than 41,000 viewers have watched this video.)

As Andy would tell you, what happened next was totally out of his control—a hands-off-the-wheel experience. He knew that eight days before the draft, many NFL teams had already zeroed in on the players they wanted. He knew there was a strong chance that he'd be left on the outside, leaning on the driver's window and looking in.

Andy was running into NFL groupthink. Some call the

NFL a "paper league" because the scouts have to justify their recommendations for draft picks to the general manager and everyone else in the organization with factual data that can be put onto paper.

Andy's pro day results, however, popped up like a jack-in-the-box. His workout numbers were faster or better than the draft's projected top three pass rushers: Chris Long, Vernon Gholston, and Derrick Harvey. Then Josh Wright whetted the teams' appetites even further by telling them that Andy was coming off an injury and was performing at just 80 percent on his pro day. He implied that if Andy had been 100 percent, his numbers would have blown up their draft projections. While some of that puffery was simply an agent working hard on behalf of his client, Wright certainly got NFL teams wondering if they needed to go rework their draft board.

For Andy to get drafted, NFL teams would have to overcome their prejudice toward Division III schools in general and Wheaton College in particular. The last time an NFL team drafted a Wheaton player was in 1957 when the Washington Redskins tabbed Fred Brock in the seventeenth round. A seventeenth-round draft pick is cannon fodder. Brock never played a down in the NFL.

A DRAFT DAY STUNNER

So how did Andy Studebaker become the surprise pick of the 2008 NFL draft—taken in the sixth round with the 203rd overall pick?

"It's funny," Andy said. "You make all these plans for your life and what it's going to look like, and the Lord has a funny way of blowing that apart and showing you who's in control and whose plans are bigger. I ended up in Philadelphia, a town I had never heard from. Funny how that works."

The Philadelphia Eagles were one of the seven teams represented at Andy's pro day. Their scout, Johnathan Stigall, helped run the workout, but he never let on to Josh Wright that the Eagles had any interest in Andy.

Eagles general manager Tom Heckert, though, was thinking of signing Andy to a free agent contract. There are now only seven rounds in the NFL draft, and GMs are loath to "waste" a pick on someone who played Division III football. But bringing in Andy as a free agent? That was doable—and low-risk.

Since teams are allowed to bring 90 players to summer training camp, general managers work quickly after the draft to fill up their dance card with undrafted free agents—sometimes within an hour or two of the final pick. Heckert, however, thought Andy would be gone before the Eagles could work out a free agent deal.

Apparently, the YouTube video was the tipping point. "Nobody ever heard of this kid, but then his workout started popping up on YouTube. The next thing you know, he got super hot," Heckert said. "We liked him, going back to his junior year when he had all those sacks. It was Division III, but he was so dominant. He was unbelievable. When he got hurt, we thought for sure he'd fall through the cracks, especially if he didn't work out [before the draft]. But once he did and the workout went on YouTube, we knew somebody else was going to take him if we didn't."

The Eagles made a preemptive strike and swooped in to

take Andy in the sixth round. His selection—at least among NFL insiders—was a stunner. Andy's pick was the highest for any Division III player since 2002.

Now he had to make the team, but it was like playing musical chairs—only a few of the extra players brought into camp had a chance of sitting in one of the 53 roster seats once the music stopped. When the final round of cuts came around just before the start of the 2008 season, the Eagles coaching staff called Andy in and gave him good news . . . and bad news. The bad news was that the Eagles were going to cut him. The good news was that the team wanted to keep him on its eight-man practice squad. "Don't leave town," the coaches said.

Andy breathed a sigh of relief. He was still part of an NFL team, and his dream of playing in the NFL was still alive. But being part of the practice team, as he would discover, was not as glamorous as it sounds. All you do is hit the weight room in the morning and practice with the team in the afternoon as part of the "look squad," the scout team that scrimmages against the starting team. You can't play in games, but you're allowed to stand on the sidelines wearing a team hat and training outfit. You don't get paid a whole lot of money, at least compared to what NFL rookies make, but you're moving in the right direction. Besides, NFL teams are also allowed to sign players off other team's practice squads, meaning there was always a chance someone wanting to see what Andy could do in a real NFL game could pick him up.

Andy's patience—a character trait his parents emphasized as he was growing up—was rewarded in Week 11 of the NFL regular season, when Josh Wright called him. His agent had a question for him: "The Kansas City Chiefs want to know if you want to play for them this Sunday. Want to go?"

Did he? Andy was on a plane the next morning. At the time, he was living with his college roommate, Javi Almanza, who'd been hired to a teaching job in Philly. Javi promised to ship Andy's clothes to Kansas City.

I asked Andy why the Kansas City Chiefs decided to pluck him off the Eagles' practice squad. "It's part of the natural cycle of the NFL," he explained. "Sometimes a team will be struggling, and they will be looking to retool with some different players. Sometimes there are injuries and holes on the roster. I didn't know at the time how long the Chiefs would want me, but hey, it was an opportunity, so I was going to take it."

Andy saw action in the last six games of the 2008 season, mainly on special teams. Unfortunately, the Chiefs were like a twenty-car pileup, finishing 2–14, the worst record in franchise history. Head coach Herm Edwards and his staff lost their jobs—and Andy wondered if he would be around the following season. "I was the last one here, so I figured I would be the first to go," he said.

The Chiefs backed up a U-Haul to their team offices and cleaned house. A new general manager, Scott Pioli, and a new head coach, Todd Haley, were the visible signs of a new regime. They valued character guys—guys willing to work hard. One of those guys, they discovered, was a young man from Wheaton College.

"I didn't know why the Chiefs brought me here, but I think I know why they've kept me," Andy said. "There's more than football in the NFL. There's relationships in the locker room, relationships in the organization, community service, and all sorts of stuff. All that is important to developing a successful team. You need character in the locker room, guys you can count on."

Andy stuck with the team as the backup to veteran Mike Vrabel, an All-Pro linebacker acquired from the New England Patriots before the 2009 season. Andy played special teams every game and saw spot action on the regular defense until . . . Vrabel got hurt in the middle of November.

"Andy, you're starting," said Gary Gibbs, his linebackers coach.

Talk about a baptism into the NFL. Coming into Kansas City that week were the Pittsburgh Steelers, Super Bowl winners the previous February with quarterback Ben Roethlisberger at the helm. The Chiefs were still NFL doormats, struggling along with a 2–7 record.

During the game, Andy picked up Steelers wide receiver Hines Ward in the flat. The pass didn't come their way, but when the play was over, Hines turned to Andy with a big smile on his face. "And you think you're going to be able to cover me?" he asked.

Of course Ward didn't think Andy could cover him, but Andy grinned back at him and answered, "Yup, I'm on you."

But then it was Andy's turn to have the last laugh. In his first NFL start, he intercepted Big Ben not once but *twice*. "Even a broken clock is right twice a day," Andy quipped.

The second interception came in the end zone, ending a long Steelers drive. Andy gathered in Roethlisberger's throw and saw lots of green real estate in front of him. He pumped his legs and zoomed up the right sideline while wide receiver

Santonio Holmes gave chase. "I thought I was being chased down, so I veered left and ended up getting tackled by another player at the 7-yard line. All I needed was three more strides, and I would have made it."

Andy's interception and 94-yard runback helped spark Kansas City's overtime upset that Sunday afternoon at Arrowhead Stadium—and led to a five-year stint with the Chiefs. "What I thought would be a short-term stay in the NFL has ended up being a decent little career," Andy said. "I'm pretty humbled."

A PROCESSION OF STUDEBAKERS

When Andy was a sophomore in college, he met Mallory Sullivan, a freshman volleyball player at Wheaton. She was an athletic 5-foot, 11-inch outside hitter, and Andy's heart fluttered every time he saw her.

Andy waited until Mallory graduated to ask for her hand in marriage, and then he came up with a wonderful surprise for the wedding, which was held in Mallory's hometown of Belleville, Illinois: leave the church amid a hail of rice and then be driven to the reception in a Studebaker Avanti, the futuristic and stylistic two-door from the 1960s.

Andy had to make a few phone calls, but a Studebaker Drivers Club in St. Louis loved his idea and said they would show up for the wedding—with not one but four Studebakers for the entire wedding party. The Studebaker Drivers Club had a long history of doing this sort of thing for weddings and special events, but this was the first time they chauffeured *real* Studebakers.

TEBOWING WITH TEBOW

In my book *Playing with Purpose: Tim Tebow*, there's an endearing photo of Andy down on one knee, holding hands and praying with a "tebowing" Tim Tebow of the Denver Broncos following the Chiefs' last regular-season game of 2011.

This was the heyday of "Tebowmania," when cameras followed Tim Tebow everywhere he went—even to the postgame prayer circles involving both teams at the 50-yard line following every Broncos contest.

Andy will one day be able to tell his grandchildren that he prayed with the man who invented tebowing—the act of dropping to one knee and offering a prayer to the Lord of the Universe. Tebowing was "invented" after a 2011 game in Miami in which Tim led the Broncos to a seemingly impossible comeback that was capped with Denver's game-winning field goal in overtime. As Matt Prater's kick sailed through the uprights, Tim genuflected, offered a prayer of thanksgiving, and pointed to the heavens.

A twenty-something Broncos fan witnessed the act on TV and thought it would be cool to take a photo of himself and his friends all on one knee, their fists against their foreheads—just as Tim had done. The photo was posted on Facebook, and faster than you can click LIKE, tebowing went viral.

So how did it happen that Andy and Tim held hands and prayed after the game?

"It was pretty random," Andy said. "I saw him at midfield, and I wanted to encourage him because I respect him a lot. Tim had a platform, and he used it well. I said to him, 'Your message now is bigger than ever,' and at the time, he totally agreed. I barely knew him, but that was a nice moment."

Andy has a platform too—smaller than that of a player as well-known as Tim Tebow, but no less important. He visits children's hospitals, reads Dr. Seuss books to elementary school children to promote reading, hosts a football camp every summer, and speaks at Fellowship of Christian Athletes events like "Fields of Faith" in the Kansas City area.

Andy has also taken part in a couple of missions trips to South Africa, where he and others worked at an orphanage a former Wheaton football player established. Andy gripped a paintbrush and laid concrete for a week. The Wheaton Football Ministry Partnership, an organization that assists Wheaton football alumni serving as missionaries in far-flung places, organized the trips. Every spring break, coaches and anyone else who wants to go join current Wheaton football players on the short-term missions trips. Andy has also participated in short-term missions trips to Romania (twice) and Senegal.

Andy says he gets much more in return from the missions trips than he gives. One time, he was out in the bush, helping members of the Zulu nation, and he could see as well as anyone else that these people had *nothing*. Yet every evening, the tribal leader would lead the people down to the riverside, where they would literally scream praises to God, thanking Him for all His gifts and mighty provision. Andy said the Zulus were the most thankful people he had ever met, and that impacted him deeply.

Two of Andy's old Wheaton football teammates currently serve in overseas mission fields, and he uses his financial resources to support them.

In a *Lion King* sort of way, that's the circle of life, isn't it?

TRAGEDY IN KANSAS CITY

I couldn't end this chapter without mentioning what happened on December 1, 2012, and how it affected Andy. On that day, his teammate and fellow linebacker Jovan Belcher murdered his girlfriend and then took his own life outside the Chiefs' practice facility at Arrowhead Stadium. (For more details, see page 240.)

Andy was driving to the stadium with a teammate when he encountered a police roadblock about a quarter of a mile from the parking lot entrance. Not long after Andy turned around his vehicle and headed away from the stadium, his teammate learned that there had been a shooting and that a Kansas City Chief was involved. Then came word that the player was Jovan Belcher, and that he had taken his own life.

The news stunned Andy. He and Belcher were more than just teammates—for two seasons, they roomed together in the team hotel the night before games. The coaches assigned roommates, and since Andy and Jovan were in the same position group, they were put together.

"We hung out, and we knew each other in meeting rooms for four years," Andy said. "This was a situation that shocked me and broke my heart. It's going to take me a while to reconcile the guy I knew, who was fun-loving, against the guy who committed those acts. It's really tough because that was not the guy I knew.

"Another reason this situation breaks my heart is because we all need to know where we can find our hope, and our hope needs to be in Jesus Christ. Football can't satisfy us, the paychecks can't, the expensive cars can't, and the things we love in this world can't sustain us.

"Only Christ can fulfill us."

4

JARED ALLEN:
MAKING MINCEMEAT OF
QUARTERBACKS

I'm not the type who normally purchases cookbooks. But when an NFL defensive lineman—especially a tough guy who has a reputation for eating quarterbacks for lunch—releases his own cookbook, then I sit up and take notice.

Jared Allen, the All-Pro Minnesota Vikings defensive end, channeled his inner Emeril and pieced together a collection of appealing recipes centered around exotic meats like buffalo, bear, elk, deer, wild boar, ostrich, pheasant, trout, and even rattlesnake. "If you're gonna eat, you oughta be willing to kill it," Jared opined in the first sentence of his tongue-in-cheek tome, *The Quarterback Killer's Cookbook*.

His cookbook is an ode to hunting, which Jared loves to do, adding that he loves nothing better than tromping through the woods with a rifle or a shotgun on his day off during the NFL season.

"Hunting is just peace, silence, a complete separation from the rest of the world," he wrote. "You're out on your own. No one bothers you. It's all about enjoying the moment, where you are and who you're with.

"Football, I train for. Hunting, I try to make time for."

Here's a rugged pioneer who could live off the land if things ever got that bad. He's a hunter, a fisherman, and one *baaad* defensive end who's every quarterback's worst nightmare. No active NFL player has more quarterback sacks than Jared Allen, save for John Abraham, who is four years older and, at the time of this writing, has played in 175 games compared with Jared's 141 games.

The Quarterback Killer's Cookbook looks to be a self-published effort, but I was pleasantly surprised at how engaging and useful it was. Jared also showed some literary chops through engaging prose that was fun to read, and his stories revealed a lot more about him than I expected. He came across as likeable, God-fearing, humorous, and sure of what it means to be manly in a culture where masculinity is devalued and often belittled.

Jared described how he grew up on various ranches in central California, why he likes eating wild, grass-fed meats so much, and how he met his wife-to-be, Amy, at his favorite restaurant, The Lodge, in the Old Town district of Scottsdale, Arizona. She was a waitress who delivered The Lodge's signature dish to his table: the 1,900-calorie Sasquatch burger, a towering combination of ground buffalo, cheese, bacon, mayo, lettuce, tomatoes, and fried onion rings set between two slices of Texas toast.

My days of wolfing down gigantic burgers are long gone, but I wanted to pay homage to Jared's culinary passions, so I decided to prepare one of his recipes on an evening when the sporting world's eyes would be upon him and the Minnesota Vikings. I waited until the first Saturday in January 2013, when the Vikings were playing the Green Bay Packers in an NFL Wild Card playoff game.

There were twenty-five recipes in the *Quarterback Killer's Cookbook*, so I had more than a few to choose from. Actually, I didn't have that much leeway because elk, bear, and rattlesnake are impossible to find in my local supermarkets. I would've had to hunt in the woods of Montana or the Minnesota wild to bag some of the animals and birds Jared described in his book.

Take for instance the recipe for "Jared's Famous Pheasant Nuggets with Country Gravy." The main ingredient was eight pheasant breasts, but pheasant season ended before Christmas in California. Plus, the local bag limit was three males per day, which would have meant three days of walking the bush with my bird dog, which, of course, I don't have. Furthermore, I hadn't hunted since I was a teenager, although I'm sure Jared would give me props for bagging a wild boar with a telescope-mounted .30-06 rifle on a New Year's Day hunt outside Santa Ynez in central California.

Jared's recipe for Duck Confit looked like a good choice, but I prefer ordering *Canard à l'Orange* in a hoity-toity white tablecloth restaurant with a French-sounding name. And I don't think I was up to eating ostrich steaks even if I could find them.

But then Jared's recipe for Buffalo Meatloaf caught my

eye. I love meatloaf, but where could I find buffalo meat?

I asked my wife, Nicole, for ideas. She wasn't sure who in town sold buffalo meat, but she was sure that Costco sold bison.

Bison? Weren't buffalo and bison one and the same? I wasn't certain, but a Google search told me that the animal commonly known as a buffalo in the U.S. is actually a bison. American bison, known for their large shoulder humps, symbolized the settling of the Old West during the wagon-train days. I knew that from watching TV westerns growing up.

Just before game time, I set my DVR to record the Vikings-Packers playoff game and then drove to Costco to do some shopping. Nicole was right: a two-pound pack of Great Range Bison, distributed by Rocky Mountain Natural Meats in Henderson, Colorado, was in the meat case and cost $13.99, or a tad less than $7 a pound. I liked how this grass-fed "home on the range" beef-like meat was raised without antibiotics and no added hormones (even though federal regulations prohibit the use of hormones in bison anyway).

As soon as I got home from Costco, I brought Jared's book over to the kitchen counter and popped it open to page 32 to get going.

"Let me make dinner," Nicole said.

"Honey, I can do this. I know I don't normally cook—"

"There's a reason for that," she retorted, "and it's because you have trouble grating a carrot."

I tried to tell Nicole that Jared didn't profess to be a cook either. "Jared said if you have meat and you have fire, you're halfway home. Besides, if you can read, you can cook," I said. "I'll manage. I can follow a recipe."

Nicole was not persuaded. "You go watch the game," she said.

Chastened, I wandered to the living room, where I worked my DVR remote and called up the Vikings playoff contest at Green Bay's Lambeau Field. The night game had started an hour earlier.

Just six days before, Minnesota had courageously beaten the Green Bay Packers in the last game of the regular season to get into the 2012 playoffs. But that was a home game played in the comfy 65 degrees of the Metrodome. Having to travel to Green Bay in January and play outdoors in 22-degree temperatures on half-frozen turf didn't portend well for the underdog Vikings.

Meanwhile, back in the kitchen, Nicole glanced through Jared's recipe, which called for two pounds of ground buffalo, or bison in our case, plus minced onion, celery, carrots, and bell pepper. As she loves telling her friends, she's never followed a recipe in her life, preferring to change ingredients to suit her taste or to add her own personal touch. For instance, Jared's ingredient list included ground-up Ritz crackers to add bulk to the meatloaf. But we don't do processed foods from Nabisco in our household. Nicole substituted Panko breadcrumbs as well as Tabasco sauce for Sriracha, a type of hot sauce from Thailand.

She combined the ingredients in a large bowl, pressed the mixture into a nonstick loaf pan, and then put the meatloaf into a 325-degree oven. That temperature seemed a little low, so Nicole turned the dial to 350 degrees. The recipe also called for baking the meatloaf for thirty minutes, pulling the loaf pan out of the oven and slathering the top of the meatloaf with ketchup, then baking it for another fifteen minutes. Nicole followed those instructions, but her eye told her the meatloaf needed to bake longer than forty-five minutes, so she raised the oven temperature to 375 degrees and let the meatloaf bake longer than the recipe called for.

So how did my wife's version of Jared Allen's Bison Meatloaf turn out?

In a word, *delicious*, although I didn't think the ketchup topping was necessary. I like my meatloaf crispy on top and prefer to add ketchup once a slice hits my plate. But that's a minor quibble. Nicole and I both commented that the bison burger tasted lean, not gamy, and we didn't leave the table feeling too full.

After cleaning up, I turned the playoff game back on just in time to see Jared sack Packers' quarterback Aaron Rodgers in the second quarter. Jared pushed around his defender and then collapsed the pocket to bring down Rodgers with a tackle around his knees. As soon as Rodgers hit the deck, Jared jumped up and celebrated the sack with a quick dip of his knees while swinging an imaginary lasso and roping an equally imaginary young calf. Jared limited his entire celebration to a second or two because he was a marked man; in 2010, the NFL warned him that the Vikings would be penalized 15 yards if he did his "lasso dance" again. Apparently, this abbreviated version didn't rise to the level of a yellow flag for excessive celebration.

If you were pulling for the Vikes to beat the Pack, like I was, that was about the only moment worth cheering. Minnesota had lost its quarterback, Christian Ponder, to an elbow injury, so little-used Joe Webb—who hadn't thrown a pass all season—got the call. Webb was ineffective. Green Bay took a commanding lead and was never challenged, winning handily, 24–10.

When the game was over, TV cameras caught Jared reaching out to Aaron Rodgers, which was nice to see, since he had been harassing him all game with his ferocious pass rush. They were, after all, friendly warriors.

For Jared, another season was in the books, and not a moment too soon. You see, Jared Allen had been playing hurt most of the season. He had a torn labrum—cartilage in his shoulder joint—and his production suffered, which raised eyebrows around the league. After dropping quarterbacks a league-leading 22 times in 2011, he had only 12 sacks during the 2012 regular season, tops on his team and eighth-best in the NFL, but not up to his lofty standards.

After the game, he told the press, "It's not good. My inside game wasn't as good as I would have liked for it to have been just because I really didn't have as much power in my hump . . . but you fight through it, and you're never fully healthy. I'll get it cleaned up."

After the Pro Bowl, he might have added. There was no way that he wasn't taking his wife, Amy, and fifteen-month-old daughter Brinley on a Hawaiian vacation. One time when he was in Oahu for the Pro Bowl, he snorkeled in a shark cage, so maybe another close encounter with a great white was in his future. Besides, the Pro Bowl was a low-intensity exhibition, nothing his bum shoulder couldn't handle.

Jared put in an appearance in Honolulu, so he got his all-expenses-paid family vacation. After Jared and his family returned to their year-round residence in Scottsdale, Arizona, he got that injured shoulder operated on. Amazingly, this was the first time he'd gone under the knife since he had his tonsils out at age five.

No knee operations in more than fifteen seasons of high school, college, and pro football? No broken bones or torn meniscus? For a football player, that's a much more remarkable stat than leading the NFL in sacks.

BRING ON BOBBY FLAY

During the start of every football telecast, the producers in the truck introduce each starter on the offense and defense during the first set of downs. You've seen this a million times, like when Tom Brady looks into the camera and says, "Tom Brady, University of Michigan."

Jared Allen likes to pull people's legs, so for one of those nationally televised Sunday night games, he looked earnestly into the camera and introduced himself in this fashion:

Jared Allen. Culinary Academy.

Celebrity chef Bobby Flay of the Food Network happened to be watching a Minnesota game one time. Intrigued, he got word to Jared that maybe he could appear on *Throwdown with Bobby Flay*, a Food Network show that features the famous chef challenging individuals to a cook-off of their signature dish.

"It'll be good television," Bobby said of pitting the Food Network star against the upstart NFL sackman.

Alas, it never worked out, so we'll never find out who makes a better braised bear.

TIME MACHINE

Jared Scot Allen is one of those larger-than-life characters a time machine (if such a thing existed) could transport into the frontier days of the Wild, Wild West and he'd fit right in.

Actually, he could go back further than that. I see him in war paint, mounted on a paint stallion, and ready to charge in the company of Mel Gibson's William Wallace in *Braveheart*.

Jared developed his warrior mentality early, living on several ranches within a hundred-mile radius in Northern California—places like Watsonville, Morgan Hill, and Gilroy, whose self-chosen moniker of "Garlic Capital the World" is well deserved.

One of the Allens' small cattle and horse ranches backed up to 3,000 open acres, which made for a huge playground for Jared and his two brothers. They shot pellet guns at doves, messed around in the creek, stalked slithering snakes, and practiced roping cattle.

Jared first went hunting with his father, Ron, and his grandfather, Ray, when he was five years old. They instructed him to carry the ammunition and keep his mouth shut.

Jared got his first introduction to where meat came from when he was in first grade as his grandfather was walking a head of cattle toward the barn. "Hey, Grandpa, what are you doing with that cow?" young Jared called out.

"You like those hamburgers we ate the other night?" Grandpa Ray asked.

"Yeah, Grandpa, I did," replied Jared.

Boom! The cow keeled over into the dirt.

"Well, that's where they come from."

Jared said that was a "pretty sweet" moment and fairly typical for his upbringing. His grandfather was a no-nonsense former Marine who served in Korea and Vietnam and packed heat 24/7. His father, cut from the same cowboy cloth, loved ridin' and ropin'. He played football at Jamestown College in

North Dakota and was good enough to be invited to the Minnesota Vikings' training camp one summer—ironic, since that's Jared's team now—but he didn't make the cut. His father went on to have a cup of coffee in the now-defunct United States Football League.

When his football days were over, Ron returned to his first loves: roping calves, riding bareback broncs in rodeos, and training horses while raising his three boys. He was their Pop Warner coach, and when Jared was eight, he told his father that he wanted to be a professional football player when he grew up. "Okay, this is what you have to do, Bud," Ron Allen told his son. "You have to eat, drink, and sleep football right now until draft day."

The Allens went through some rough patches as Jared was growing up, including a period of time when they lived in a trailer and had only Kraft Macaroni & Cheese to eat for dinner. But they muddled their way through, and Jared learned many valuable lessons living on a ranch. One of those lessons was that the chores never went away. Jared mucked his share of stalls and painted his share of fencing growing up.

Meanwhile, Jared grew like a young Angus bull. In high school, he was a big, rawboned kid—a 6-foot, 6-inch, 240-pound mass of hewn muscle. He was making a name for himself on the football field at Live Oak High in Morgan Hill when he got caught up in a stupid yearbook prank. Some yearbooks went missing, fingers were pointed at Jared as being one of the ringleaders, and the principal suggested that he find another school.

Jared's parents were divorced, so he went to live with his mother, Sarah, in nearby Los Gatos. Now he had to prove himself to a brand new set of coaches as well as college recruiters, who like to see continuity in a player. A senior year transfer is a red flag to college recruiters, and whispers that he was a bit of a hellion extinguished any interest from Division I colleges like Stanford, Michigan State, Colorado, and Washington.

Only one Division I-AA school offered Jared a scholarship—Idaho State University in Pocatello. He made Big Sky Conference quarterbacks rue the day he enrolled. He chased them all over the field and ground them into the dirt whenever he got his big ranch hands on them.

The first fissures of bad behavior were starting to leak out in college, however. In one run-in with the law, he was busted for alcohol consumption as well as resisting arrest. The courts took away his driver's license for thirty days, and the Bengals suspended him from spring practice. When he came back for his senior season, though, he played spectacularly, winning the 2003 Buck Buchanan Award as the top Division I-AA defensive player.

At 6 foot, 6 inches tall but now 265 pounds, Jared, who also ran the 40 in 4.64 seconds, had NFL scouts practically salivating at the prospect of having him as a sack-maker. But what about the character issues? Just as good character helped a Division I-AA player like Corey Lynch make it to the NFL, questions about character nearly sank Jared's chances to play in the pros. He slipped to the fourth round of the 2004 NFL draft before the Kansas City Chiefs took a flyer on him. Some coaches in the Chiefs' organization thought he was best suited as a long snapper, but his brilliant talent as a defensive player showed up like a klieg light on the practice field. The idea of turning him into a long-snapper on special teams was quickly and quietly shelved.

Jared, installed at defensive end, started ten games his rookie year and led the Chiefs with nine sacks. The sack parade continued, and during his third year in the league, in 2006, Jared led the NFL with 15½ sacks. He was on the fast track to stardom, but his path to true happiness was blocked by something he enjoyed but couldn't handle—partying.

Jared had gone to church some growing up, but he was a drifting soul throughout much of college and his early years in the NFL. He was the social animal who pronounced *parr-tee* with two r's. He was the fun-loving guy who showed up at a Chiefs' team meeting one Halloween wearing a Speedo, goggles, and six gold medals around his neck as part of his Michael Phelps "costume." (The gold medals were actually gold-foiled chocolate coins.)

He was also the guy who skydived in Arizona, ran with the bulls at Pamplona, Spain, and zip-lined through the rain forest of Costa Rica during the off-season. Even his first love, hunting, had to be top-of-the-top experiences. He took a trip to New Zealand in search of red stags, and one time he crept up commando-style on a 200-pound wild boar, clenching a Bowie hunting knife, which he used to stab and kill the beast.

However, Jared didn't enjoy these great experiences in a vacuum. As often happens with young men in their twenties, flush with cash and egos stroked by fame, Jared didn't know when to say enough was enough. "I was twenty-two and single when I got in the league," he said. "They told me to go out, play football, and have fun. I was like, *Okay, I can do that.*"

Then there was the image Jared projected. The Samsonian

trail of hair behind his ears told the world that he was "rocking a mullet"—a hairstyle that was "business up front, party in the back." Mullets may have had their heyday back in the mid-1980s, but Jared didn't care. His flowing locks became part of his tough guy persona and made him a subject of conversation on fan blogs.

Burning the party candle at both ends finally caught up with Jared. In 2006, he was arrested for *two* DUIs, his second coming during the middle of the season after he had broken up with a college sweetheart and had drowned his sorrows at a Kansas City-area bar. He climbed behind the wheel of his Dodge truck to drive home. He swerved across lanes of traffic . . . until a cop nailed him—possibly preventing a tragedy.

Jared continued playing while awaiting a February court date. After Jared entered a plea of no contest to the charges, the judge sentenced him to two days in jail. There was something about being incarcerated that got Jared's attention. Then the hammer came down from the NFL commissioner's office. Roger Goodell suspended Jared for the first four games of the 2007 season (the suspension was later reduced to two games on appeal), prompting Chiefs general manager Carl Peterson to hold back from offering Jared a long-term contract. "He's a very good football player, but a young man at risk," Peterson said.

In other words, *We've got character issues.*

Even though spending two days in a Kansas county slammer was a jolt, it was Jared's grandfather who finally got through to him.

"I told him, 'You're screwing up this family's name. Now what are you going to do about it?' " said Ray Allen, who was in his late seventies at the time. "I said, 'If you want to be the best, then start acting like the best. It's time to be a football player only. You can't be the town drunk.' "

Jared decided to quit drinking—cold turkey. And he decided to get a lot more serious about God. In a team chapel, he heard a question that changed his life: *If you were arrested for being a Christian today, would there be enough evidence to convict you?*

"My answer was no," he told an interviewer with the Christian Broadcasting Network. "On an outwardly basis, the world could not convict me as a Christian, even though I knew where my heart was. Everyone says that's the most important thing, and it is. But let's be honest: You have to walk the walk."

That new walk started with baby steps. Jared knew he couldn't rush the Deceiver and take him down on his own; he needed the Lord lining up next to him—a double team, if you will.

"When you think you're outnumbered, God's got your back. He says He's always there with you," he said. "If I don't get a sack every game, that doesn't mean I want to quit football. It makes me want to work harder. If I don't read my playbook, I'm not successful on the field. My Bible is my playbook for life. If I don't read my Bible, how can I stand firm and wear the full armor of Christ and stand firm against the world if I don't know what's there?"

MOVE TO MINNESOTA

While Jared was working through his "issues," the Kansas City Chiefs had a decision to make. In 2007, Jared was in the last year of his contract, but because of his off-the-field troubles, general manager Carl Peterson was reluctant to ink him to a long-term deal. The Chiefs organization was waiting to see how the season would play out.

Wary of becoming a cautionary tale of what goes wrong for a young NFL player, Jared tended to business during the 2007 season, sticking to non-alcoholic O'Doul's beer when he socialized with his teammates and concentrating on beating the O-line to the quarterback when he was on the football field. He led the NFL in two huge categories: "pressures," which means he was in the quarterback's personal space more than anyone in the NFL; and sacks, where he registered a career-high 15½ in only fourteen games. (Remember, he lost two games due to the NFL suspension.)

Staying in character, Jared shaved notches—"racing stripes," he called them—into his prized mullet each time he sacked a quarterback. He also displayed a knack for coming up with big plays from his defensive end position. When the season was over, he received his first Pro Bowl invitation.

Jared was too good a player to be cast overboard into the sea of free agency, so Peterson slapped the "franchise tag" on him, meaning he would be paid the average salary of the league's five highest-paid players at his position, which was close to $9 million a year. The franchise tag has been likened to golden handcuffs, though, because without the tag, Jared would have been allowed to test the free agent market to find out what he was really worth.

During the off-season, the Minnesota Vikings were looking to fill a hole at defensive end. Their front office surveyed the league and scoured the free agent listings. They were interested in Jared, but he wasn't a free agent. If he was to become a

Viking, the team would have to broker a trade.

Minnesota defensive coordinator Leslie Frazier knew Jared had been arrested for drunk driving three times since 2002. Was he still on the wagon? Was he a changed man? If not, he was one strike away from a year-long suspension from the NFL.

Then again, there was a lot of talent to like. Jared created sacks without secondary blitzes, batted down passes, stopped the run, and harassed every quarterback put in front of him. Offenses *had* to scheme against him.

At the Pro Bowl, former Vikings fullback Tony Richardson spent time talking with Jared, his former Chiefs teammate. Richardson later told the Vikings front office that he was impressed by Jared's attitude and personal growth. As trade discussions intensified, the Vikings summoned Jared to Minneapolis to meet with the big brass: owner Zygi Wilf, vice president of player personnel Rick Spielman, head coach Brad Childress, and Leslie Frazier.

"I wanted to see if this guy was a con artist," Frazier said bluntly, "or if he was a guy just out for himself and not about the team. But after spending time around him, I realized he's what you want in a teammate. He's a solid, solid person who made some mistakes in his life and stood up and atoned for them."

The Vikings pulled the trigger on a blockbuster trade-and-sign deal: a truckload of draft picks (a first-rounder and two third-rounders) and a monster $74 million, six-year contract that included $31 million in guarantees. It was the biggest contract ever extended to a player on the defensive side of the ball.

Five years into the deal, Jared has held up his side of the bargain. He *almost* set the single-season sack record in 2011 despite being double-teamed much of the year. His 22 sacks were just half a sack short of the season record set by Michael Strahan of the New York Giants in 2001, leaving the ultra-competitive Jared a bit miffed because one quarterback drop was recorded and then erased.

"They actually took one away from me in Green Bay," Jared said. "I pushed my guy into [Aaron] Rodgers, he fumbled, and I touched him down. They gave it as a team sack, versus giving me the sack. That would've been the record right there."

Then there was the fact that Strahan's record-breaking sack was the subject of some controversy. Strahan was a good friend of Brett Favre, then with the Green Bay Packers. During the Giants' final game of the 2001 season—against the Packers—Strahan set the record on a play when Favre appeared to intentionally take the sack. Strahan practically walked into the Packer offensive backfield as Favre hit the deck. Strahan lightly fell on top of him to collect the NFL record.

As Jared said after just missing the NFL record, "It's like being runner-up at the prom." But he's still got time. As of the start of the 2013 season, Jared was only thirty-one, so he still has a few more years left as a top-flight defensive lineman.

Jared is maturing. The signature mullet is gone, having been snipped off in the spring of 2010, just before his wedding to Amy Johnson. "The things men do for love," he said.

Let's not hear any Delilah jokes.

Jared finished *The Quarterback Killer's Cookbook* with

this open-ended invitation: "The next time you're in Scotts-dale, look me up at The Lodge. I'll be there if I'm not out hunting ball carriers or wild boar. All depends on what's in season."

I haven't been to Scottsdale in years, but maybe Nicole will split one of those Sasquatch burgers with me. It'd be worth a try.

Or maybe Jared will be hanging out with his hunting buddies at his favorite table. I wouldn't ask him for his auto-graph, but I will want to want to know when his next cook-book is coming out.

PASS RUSHING 101 WITH JARED ALLEN

Why is Jared Allen so good at what he does?

You start with his body, which is long and lanky for someone so big. There's no paunch resting on the beltline of his slotted pants. His broad shoulders taper nicely to a narrow waistline—the product of years in the gym improving his core strength, lifting his endurance, boosting hip flexibility, and working on his hand-eye coordination.

When the ball is snapped, Jared gets off the line like a puma. He's so fast that he can catch running backs before they hit the hole. He can chase down screen passes. If the quarterback settles into the pocket and waits a tad too long to get rid of the ball, then he finds out that Jared hits like a fifth-wheel truck.

Keep in mind that where Jared plies his trade is in hand-to-hand combat. Gone are the days when defensive ends like Deacon Jones could head-slap offensive tackles to gain an advantage. In today's game, technique is just as important as strength, desire, and attitude. He studies game film year-round to pick up footwork and stance tendencies of his offensive counterparts. He expects to be double-teamed.

Jared shared some "rules for the rush" on Stack TV (stack.com), which are summarized here:

General notes:

• Angle your hips toward the quarterback. Wherever your hips are going, you're going.

• With all rushes, it's imperative to gain as much ground as possible with your first step.

• Make sure you make contact with the tackle by your third step.

Alignment:

• Get as close to the line of scrimmage as possible without being offsides.

• Align 1½ to 2 yards outside of the tackle.

• Angle your body toward where the quarterback will be on his drop.

Stance:

• Place ball-side leg back and other leg forward.

• Keep your feet shoulder-width apart.

• Place your weight on your front foot.

• Put your ball-side hand on ground.

Jared employs several different rushes: a speed rush for when the tackle sets to his inside; a hump rush, when the tackle sets to his outside; a bull rush when the tackle sets directly in front of him; and a single-hand and double-hand rush to break free of the tackle's block.

The next time you watch a Minnesota Vikings game, study Jared's technique for getting past his man and slipping off a block and tackling a running back.

It's all part of the game within a game.

5

PHIL DAWSON:
SPLITTING GOD'S UPRIGHTS

I've had the privilege of writing a lot of books, and one of my first collaborative efforts was *Alive & Kicking*, the autobiography of Rolf Benirschke, a placekicker with the San Diego Chargers in the late 1970s and early 1980s.

If you've been a football fan long enough, you might recognize Rolf's name because of a kick that defined his career: his field goal that decided what many football experts call one of the greatest playoff games ever—the Chargers' 41–38 overtime defeat of the Miami Dolphins in an AFC divisional playoff game on January 2, 1982.

For nearly five quarters, the Chargers and the Dolphins played a game of "Can you top this?" It appeared that the two offenses couldn't be stopped if you dug a moat at the line of scrimmage. The two teams combined to generate more than 1,000 yards in total offense and produced enough highlight reel performances to fill ESPN's "Top 10 Plays of the Day."

Early in *Alive & Kicking*, Rolf described how the Oakland Raiders selected him in the 12th and final round of the 1977 NFL draft (there were a dozen rounds back then). Since Rolf was the 334th out of 335 players picked, his prospects for landing an NFL kicking job weren't considered good.

Back in 1977, the Raiders were the reigning Super Bowl champs. They were the feared "Silver and Black" and featured personalities like Kenny "The Snake" Stabler, John "The Tooz" Matuszak, and bald, tough-looking Otis Sistrunk, who, as one TV color man joked, had graduated from the University of Mars. John Madden—yes, the Madden of the *Madden NFL* video games—coached this cast of colorful characters.

Madden was a bit of an eccentric himself. He had a reputation for not liking rookies *or* kickers, which made Rolf just about his least favorite player on the team. It was nothing personal; he just didn't care for players who didn't get their uniforms dirty.

Madden, who seemed to enjoy making life miserable for kickers, was famous for his little "tests." One week into the 1977 summer training camp, Rolf received his first exam. As morning practice was coming to a close, Madden pulled the entire team together.

"Gentlemen, as you all know, we end each practice by running ten sideline-to-sideline sprints," the rumpled coach bellowed. "Today, we're going to find out how good our rookie kicker is. Benirschke, you've got one shot from 45 yards. If you make it, everyone hits the showers. If you miss, everyone runs."

Madden hadn't warned Rolf about his test, so he was totally unprepared. His stomach executed a backflip as he considered the repercussions of an errant field goal attempt. Then the catcalls rained down from the sidelines. "Hey rook, you better not miss this @#$% kick!" yelled John Matuszak.

Rolf had to kick against a live rush. While the rest of the players were going crazy on the sidelines, yelling at him to make the field goal if he knew what was good for him, back-up quarterback David Humm took a knee at the 45-yard line, seven yards behind the line of scrimmage. "You can make this sucker," he said to Rolf as he smoothed out the ground.

As Rolf paced off the steps for his approach, the noise level grew. He willed his beating heart to slow down and tried to make himself feel comfortable and in control. The ball was snapped, and Humm put it down and spun the football so that the laces faced away from his kicker. At the same time, Rolf was already striding toward the ball. He planted his left foot and swung with his right . . . effortlessly. The leather ball spun end-over-end toward the goalposts and easily cleared the cross bar. The kick was good!

The players, ecstatic that they didn't have to run wind sprints, whooped and hollered. Rolf exhaled, but he didn't feel any joy, only relief.

That was not the last time John Madden would test Rolf. Even though he would make every pressure kick in practice, Rolf grew to despise Madden for his pop quizzes. But the wily coach had prepared him for the fierce pressure NFL kickers face every Sunday.

Placekickers are specialists operating in a laboratory of intense duress. Their tension-filled, singular job sounds simple: stride toward a football set on the ground by their holder, kick the ball with the instep of their foot, and send it cleanly through the goalposts. The kick must be long enough and high enough to pass over a ten-foot-high cross bar and accurate enough to stay inside vertical posts that are 18 feet, 6 inches apart and extend thirty feet above the cross bar. A ribbon four inches wide and 42 inches long is attached to the top of each post, giving kickers an idea of wind direction. Swirling breezes can greatly affect the distance and direction of a kick.

Placekicking is a tremendously important part of football. The fact is that two great teams can battle each other in the trenches for 59 minutes and 59 seconds, but the gladiators must leave the game's outcome in the hands—make that the foot—of a diminutive player weighing 160 pounds who trots out to kick a field goal. With a sweep of his leg, the game is won, lost, or tied.

Since nearly a quarter of all NFL contests are decided by three points or less, the significance of the placekicker's role can't be underestimated. It always seems like the bigger the game, the more likely victory or defeat will be decided by a place kick lofted toward those uprights ten yards deep in the end zone.

Kicking field goals with the game on the line is not for the faint of heart, which is why placekicking is one of the most nerve-wracking vocations in all of sport. Mental toughness is a prerequisite—and so is a short memory for kicks gone awry. Often, the fate of an NFL team's season comes down to a snap, a hold, and a kick.

THROWING SNOWBALLS

When I related Rolf's story to Phil Dawson, who kicked fourteen years for the Cleveland Browns before signing with San Francisco prior to the 2013 season, all he could do was laugh and ruefully shake his head. "When I started out with the

Browns in the late '90s, there was still a bit of that mentality among coaches—the mentality that they had to see if their kicker could handle the pressure," he said.

Phil faced a similar challenge during his rookie camp in 1999. At the end of one practice that summer, he looked to the side and noticed several equipment managers rolling up pairs of white tube socks and binding them with adhesive tape. Then he heard Browns head coach Chris Palmer announce a final drill involving the field goal unit.

Phil was directed to line up for a field goal near the 40-yard line. Surrounding the field goal unit were dozens of sweaty players. Coach Palmer directed them to throw the rolled-up socks at Phil as he attempted a "game-winning" kick.

"It was called the Snowball Drill," Phil said. "Literally, while I was lining up for the kick, I was getting pelted in the head, getting hit in the chest. The holder was getting hit. Guys were trying to hit the ball as it came out of the snapper's hands."

While the players were lobbing sock snowballs at Phil and his holder, they were also laughing their heads off and having a good time. Meanwhile, you could fry an egg on Phil's generous forehead.

"I remember getting pretty frustrated," he said. "This Snowball Drill was just so unrealistic to me. I had a job to do and work that needed to get done, but throwing rolled-up socks at me was getting in the way. Sure, I made the kick and earned my stripes, but it felt like practice was serious for everyone but the kicker."

Phil finds it interesting that coaches often single out placekickers for these prickly examinations at the close of practice. "The last time I checked, the quarterback still has to make the throw on fourth-and-eight, and the receiver still has to make the catch," he said. "Kickers are certainly not the only players on the field who have to execute at a critical moment, but for whatever reason, kickers are singled out. In the last decade, though, these training camp tests have died down. Interestingly, we've seen field goal percentages and production from kickers dramatically increase."

Are they related?

"I think so," Phil answered. "I would argue that many kickers through the years were so worn down from all the tests during the week that they couldn't possibly engage in the way they needed to from a mental toughness standpoint once the game started. Fortunately for me, there haven't been a whole lot of those tests in my career."

That was interesting to hear because Phil Dawson and his bionic leg seem to get better with age. During the 2012 season, at the age of 37, Phil nailed 29 of 31 field goal attempts for a 93.5 conversion rate, good for second in the NFL. He also didn't miss an extra point. Through the first twelve games of the Cleveland Browns' season, he didn't miss a field goal attempt and had made 29 consecutive attempts—including six from 50 yards or further—between the 2011 and 2012 seasons. He finally got some well-deserved recognition when he was voted to his first Pro Bowl at the end of the 2012 season.

THE ANNOUNCER'S CURSE

Thanks to NFL RedZone, I was able to follow a lot of the players featured in the NFL edition of *Playing with Purpose* during the 2012 season.

Of course, I used my DVR to tape seven hours of NFL

RedZone and speed through the action late on Sunday. I liked stopping the fast-forward button on my remote every time Phil Dawson lined up for a field goal because it was fun to watch him make them all. Going into Week 13 against the Oakland Raiders, he was a perfect 21 for 21 on the season.

That factoid gave the CBS announcers that day, Bill Macatee and Steve Tasker, something to kibitz about as two unremarkable teams with 3–8 records squared off in Oakland. Rain showers pelting the Bay Area over the weekend had turned the grassy field into a swamp.

After Phil made his first two field goal attempts, Macatee suggested he had a chance to go the entire season without missing—which would make Phil the seventh kicker in NFL history to accomplish the feat. Meanwhile, the sloppy field looked like a good place to stage a mud-wrestling event. Then, a Browns drive stalled near the Raiders goal line.

"Anything inside the 20-yard line is going to be iffy," Macatee intoned as the Browns lined up for a 28-yard attempt. "The long ones are easy, but the footing is so bad at this end of the field."

The snap was a bit low, and Phil's kick was deflected at the line of scrimmage. The ball wobbled through the air like a wounded duck and missed wide left.

"And the streak comes to an end," said Macatee. "I have to apologize for bringing it up before he hit that kick."

The dreaded announcer's curse strikes again.

RedZone anchorman Scott Hanson chimed in over the game feed from Oakland, "Phil Dawson's first miss of the season, and it was a chip shot."

Phil knew the kick was going to be trouble since that end of the field was a gooey mess. With the Browns facing a fourth-and-four, he tried to quickly suggest that the offense attempt to lure the Raiders offside. If their defense didn't jump on the snap count, then the Browns could take a delay-of-game penalty, which would mean Phil could kick from a spot on the field where the turf wasn't as chewed up.

"I caught everyone off guard. There wasn't enough time to get the offense back out there," Phil said. "I had to kick out of the soup. It was tough on the guys in front. They tried to stab their cleats in the mud, but they couldn't get a hold, so they got pushed back. The ball came out a little lower than it should have, so it was just a perfect storm for the block.

"I missed one other field goal in the last game of the season at Heinz Field in Pittsburgh," Phil added. "That keeps me hungry. I've always wanted to go the entire season without missing one. I almost got it done last year. Now I've got something to shoot for this season."

That was nice to see for someone who's labored in near anonymity kicking for a team that made the NFL playoffs only once during his long tenure with the Browns.

What makes Phil's lengthy kicking career even more amazing is that until the 2013 season, he plied his trade inside the toughest venue in the NFL—Cleveland Browns Stadium (now known as FirstEnergy Stadium). Swirling, frosty winds whisk off nearby Lake Erie and whip through the stadium bowl, prodding blue-collar fans in the east end zone to hold on to their Dawg Pound headgear with both hands. After Halloween, the natural grass turf goes dormant and the field becomes a soft, moist morass that looks like painted dirt in green hues. Icy temperatures numb the spirit beyond the Ides of November.

If Phil ever needed confirmation on how tough it was to kick in Cleveland, he received it following every home game. After the final seconds would tick off, kickers from both teams would seek each other out in the middle of the field. The first thing the visiting team's kicker said to Phil was something like, "Man, I don't know how you kick here."

"They also said, 'Boy, am I glad I don't have to come back,' " Phil added. "I appreciated the sentiment, but they only played in Cleveland once a year. I kicked in Cleveland eight times a year, and that had a cumulative effect on you. People ask me why I'm bald now. I tell them that kicking in Cleveland for fourteen years will tear your hair out pretty quickly."

So how did Phil Dawson end up kicking for the Cleveland Browns, an expansion franchise in 1999 after owner Art Modell moved the original Browns to Baltimore in 1996 and rechristened the team the Baltimore Ravens?

Answer: through a single-minded work ethic and a commitment to make kicking a football between a pair of uprights a thoroughly professional endeavor. Phil looks at placekicking as a craft and a skill that must be constantly honed through practice, patience, and polish. He's succeeded in a way that's as straight and true as one of his end-over-end kicks from 50 yards.

BIGFOOT ON THE LOOSE

Except for a "gap year" during his freshman year of college, Philip Drury Dawson has followed the straight and true path all his life. You can credit Christian parents who not only taught him and his younger brother Peter the difference between right and wrong, but who also modeled that behavior.

One of the life lessons Robert and Judy Dawson instilled in Philip—as he was known all the way through high school—was this: *Just don't work hard to work hard, but work hard because God wants you to and wants you to honor Him with the opportunities He gives you.*

Phil saw his parents live out their faith in the way they handled tough financial times. Dad was an accountant and Mom was a real estate agent who sold homes in their Lake Highlands neighborhood in northeast Dallas. In the late 1980s, when Philip was a high school freshman, the residential real estate market took a nosedive—and so did the family income.

Phil remembers well how his parents demonstrated their faith and determination during one particularly tough Christmas season.

"It was the holiday season, and Mom couldn't bear the thought that my brother and I wouldn't have any gifts at Christmas," Phil said. "She took a night job at Gap to earn some money and receive the employee discount. Every gift that Peter and I got that Christmas was from Gap, but that was Mom. I'm sure she took full satisfaction knowing that she could do that for us. Sure, Christmas was rather subdued, but to this day, especially being older now, I feel like that was my favorite Christmas.

"Mom could have stayed home complaining about her lot in life or questioning God, but instead of doing that, she went out and worked hard to give us a Christmas. Dad was grinding away, too, working Christmas Eve and just taking Christmas Day off. They both figured out ways to make sure that my brother and I were loved and cared for. They were such a great example to me."

Phil's first foray into organized sports was in soccer, a game four-year-olds can actually play. From his very first practice, he showed a strong leg, inspiring his coach—his father—to come up with a game plan for their peewee league.

"You go down by the other goal," Robert said, pointing to

the goal their team had to defend. "When you get the chance, kick the ball as far as you can. Then Brian can score."

There was no offside rule in peewee soccer, so having Brian waiting down by the other team's goal turned out to be a winning strategy. When the ball came loose on the defensive end, Phil would boom the ball in Brian's direction, and what happened next was almost a penalty kick situation since Brian was one-on-one with the goalie.

As Phil worked his way through various youth soccer leagues, he earned a nickname that evoked his special talent: Bigfoot. If your team needed a player who could kick the soccer ball a long way, Phil was your guy.

Phil wasn't just a soccer player growing up; he played all team sports, including baseball and basketball. He started playing Pop Warner football in seventh grade and put his sturdy frame to good use at fullback and linebacker. At the end of preseason practice, his coach called everyone to the sidelines.

"Our first game is next Saturday," the coach began, "and we need to figure out who's going to punt and kick off. Any takers?"

Everyone looked at Bigfoot.

"Philip, you need to do it," piped up one teammate.

"Yeah, everyone knows how far you can kick," commented another.

Phil was game—he couldn't let down his teammates, of course—and that is how he started kicking a football. But he didn't kick field goals or extra points that first year since a long snap, a hold, and a kick was a little too sophisticated for Pop Warner football. But he certainly got a lot of practice kicking off the tee each time his team scored a touchdown,

Corey Lynch, pictured with his wife, Cissie, played safety for the San Diego Chargers during the 2012 season. He's also a highly regarded special teams player noted for his ability to block punts and field goal attempts. (Photo courtesy of Corey Lynch)

During the 2012 season, Corey Lynch intercepted two passes while appearing in all 16 games and starting the last four for the San Diego Chargers.
(AP Photo/Ric Tapia)

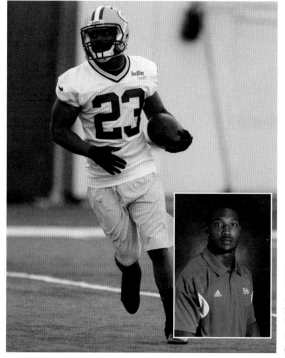

God used a UCLA janitor to get a hold of Johnathan Franklin when he was running for the UCLA Bruins. After giving his life to Christ, Johnathan became a spiritual leader on the team. Now he's taken his swift moves to the NFL, where he's in the Green Bay Packers backfield. When Johnathan's playing days are over, he has political aspirations, including one day being elected mayor of Los Angeles.
(AP Photo / Mike Roemer; inset photo courtesy of UCLA)

In a Monday night game on October 31, 2011, Andy Studebaker celebrates the recovery of a fumble by Philip Rivers, quarterback of the San Diego Chargers. (AP Photo/Ed Zurga)

During the height of Tebowmania that defined the 2011 season, Andy Studebaker clasped Tim Tebow's hand when players from both sides met at the 50-yard line following the game to pray. (AP Photo/Jack Dempsey)

San Diego Chargers chaplain and former Chargers running back Terrell Fletcher and his wife, Sheree, are involved in a thriving multicultural ministry at City of Hope International Church in San Diego, where Terrell is the senior pastor and Sheree heads up the women's ministry efforts. (Terrell Fletcher photo)

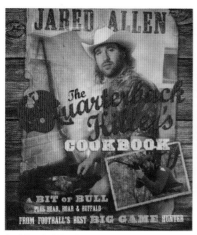

Jared Allen, the 6-foot, 6-inch rushing tank for the Minnesota Vikings, is every quarterback's nightmare . . . and the author of a cookbook. This is the cover for *The Quarterback Killer's Cookbook*, Jared's collection of man-hungry recipes centered around exotic meats like buffalo, bear, elk, deer, wild boar, ostrich, pheasant, trout—even rattlesnake.

When the ball is snapped, Minnesota Vikings defensive end Jared Allen pounces like a puma. Few offensive linemen can keep him away from the quarterback for more than four seconds.
(AP Photo/G. Newman Lowrance)

Tampa Bay Buccaneers head coach Greg Schiano saw one of his players—Eric LeGrand—go down when Schiano was coaching at Rutgers University in 2010. A frightening collision left the young student paralyzed from the neck down and bound to a wheelchair. Eric's disability, however, didn't stop Coach Schiano from signing him to a free agent contract with the Bucs, a humanitarian gesture that warmed the hearts of football fans everywhere. **(AP Photo/Brian Blanco)**

When it comes to making field goals, Phil Dawson—a long-time kicker with the Cleveland Browns now playing for the San Francisco 49ers—is dedicated to his craft. He received some well-deserved recognition when he was voted to his first Pro Bowl at the end of the 2012 season. During pregame warm-ups in Honolulu, he posed with his wife, Shannon, and their three children (from left): Beau, Sophiann, and Dru. **(Photo courtesy of Phil Dawson)**

Phil Dawson kicked fourteen seasons with the Cleveland Browns, ranking as the tenth-most accurate field-goal kicker in NFL history. That's quite an achievement, since he kicked half his games on Cleveland's chewed-up grass field. **(AP Photo / Tom DiPace)**

Since he led the New Orleans Saints to a Super Bowl victory in 2010, Drew Brees draws cameras everywhere he goes. The popular quarterback became the face of New Orleans following the mass destruction of Hurricane Katrina, and the Brees Dream Foundation has helped raise money for revitalization projects in the Big Easy. **(Photo courtesy of Mike Yorkey)**

Sam Bradford has showed flashes of brilliance during his first three seasons quarterbacking the St. Louis Rams, but his fans are still waiting for the breakout season. **(AP Photo/G. Newman Lowrance)**

Tim Tebow's career as an NFL quarterback may be hanging by a football lace with the New England Patriots, but as he is quick to tell anyone, God is in control and has a plan for his life. Will his future be in speaking? On Father's Day in 2012, Tim shared his heart before 26,000 at San Diego's Qualcomm Stadium. **(Photo courtesy of Mike Yorkey)**

Colt McCoy is pictured at Darrel K Royal-Texas Memorial Field with his wife, Rachel, and his father, Brad. Colt had his No. 12 Longhorns jersey retired and wore the same number during his NFL stay in Cleveland. Now, in San Francisco, he's #2—backing up 49er quarterback Colin Kaepernick. **(AP Photo/Jeff Chiu; Mike Yorkey)**

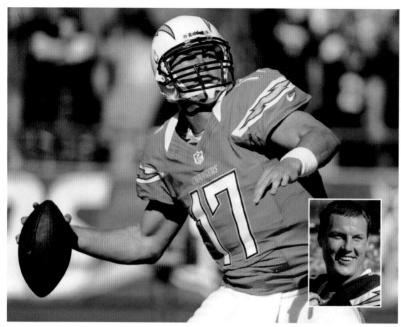

There are few deep threats greater than San Diego Chargers quarterback Philip Rivers, who can heave the ball downfield with the best of them. **(AP Photo/Denis Poroy)**

(Insert) Philip Rivers, one of pro football's elite quarterbacks with the San Diego Chargers, leads the NFL in one noteworthy category: the number of children with one wife. He and Tiffany are the proud parents of six children. **(Photo courtesy of Philip Rivers)**

At the end of the 2012 season, Christian Ponder was in a hurry: He used his off-day to marry Samantha Steele, a reporter and host for ESPN college football. Christian had a superb season in 2012 in leading the Vikings back to the playoffs. **(AP Photo/Nam Y. Huh)**

San Francisco 49ers quarterback Colin Kaepernick came out of nowhere to lead the Niners to the Super Bowl in 2013 with his speedy feet and laser-like throws. **(AP Photo/Paul Jasienski)**

which happened often. He really put his foot into his punts, and they traveled a long way.

Phil's coaches told his parents that his impressive leg could take him places. Word of Phil's kicking prowess filtered up to the coaches at Lake Highlands High School, who wrangled him an invitation to a kicking camp run by Dallas Cowboys kicking coach Ben Agajanian, a legend in kicking circles. Agajanian, who kicked for twenty seasons in the NFL and the old AFL, was known as the "Toeless Wonder" because, during his college years, the toes of his kicking foot had been amputated after they were crushed in a freight elevator accident. He overcame that handicap to become pro football's first kicking specialist in the post-war years of the 1940s.

"That kicking camp was mostly comprised of graduating seniors from high school who were getting ready to try out for a college team," Phil said. "I don't know how I got into that camp since I was a ninth grader still in junior high, but I ended up not just holding my own but doing pretty well in the competition. At the end of that camp, Coach Agajanian approached my parents and said, 'I would really like to start working with Phil. He has a bright future and natural abilities in this area, and he really needs to pursue placekicking.' "

Phil listened politely and would ultimately work with Coach Agajanian, but going into high school, he saw himself as a *football player*, not just a kicker. He wanted to be involved in blocking and tackling and making plays on offense or defense, not just jogging onto the field after a touchdown or when his team needed a field goal. He wasn't ready to become a specialist just yet.

The trouble is that his powerful leg could not be overlooked.

Playing on the ninth-grade team, Phil made his only field-goal attempt of the season—a 49-yarder. He won a roster spot on the varsity his sophomore year but didn't see much action. During his junior year, though, he started at offensive tackle and also handled the kicking duties. He hit his first 50-yarder that season, but it was a pair of game-winning field goals during his senior year that had college scouts beating a path to the Dawson residence with scholarship offers in hand: a 53-yarder against Richardson High in the game's final seconds and a 52-yarder on the game's final play against Nacogdoches in the 1992 state playoffs.

GOOFY FOOT

Phil Dawson is really messed up.

Please let me explain.

Phil kicks right-footed, but if his holder fumbles the long snap and Phil picks up the ball to make a desperation pass, he'd throw with his *left* hand.

But Phil writes right-handed. Yet he swings a baseball bat and a golf club left-handed (and plays to a 7 handicap). Wait a minute—he plays tennis right-handed, including the serve. He also shoots a shotgun right-handed.

Phil is not ambidextrous, however. If you put a baseball in his right hand to play catch, you might tease him for throwing like a girl. The only thing Phil does from both sides is kick field goals.

The sight of Phil alternating legs with his PATs would be quite a sight, something to get the football pundits at ESPN yapping. It's doubtful he'll ever get the chance, though.

"That's when I started blowing up in college recruiting and the whole deal," Phil said. "I was fortunate to play at a high school where there were a lot of college recruiters. Who knows if anyone would have noticed me if I played anywhere else."

Sure, playing under the bright Friday night lights of Texas high school football certainly helped Phil's prospects for playing college football, but hitting game-winners from beyond the midfield stripe made it clear that Phil had a special talent for kicking the ball in pressure-packed situations.

But many college football programs are loathe to offer scholarships to placekickers. Instead, they host tryouts every summer, inviting "walk-ons" (players who try to make the team without the benefit of a scholarship) to show what they can do. That was not the situation Phil faced.

"I was offered full rides to a lot of different places, including the University of Texas, which is where I always wanted to go," Phil said. "I was fortunate because a lot of kickers don't have that opportunity. Many have to prove themselves before being offered a scholarship. The reason more universities don't grant scholarships and force guys to try out is because there's very little understanding about kicking among coaches in the football world. In fact, they will admit that they know nothing about kicking. You can go to these coaches' clinics, and there will be seminars on every aspect about football except for kicking.

"I still haven't figured this part out, but it's acceptable in the football world to not know anything about kicking. The reason why coaches are reluctant to hand out a valued scholarship is because they really don't know what to look for in a recruit. If it's the quarterback position, they know what to look for. *Does he have good feet? What's his arm like? Can he throw to the sideline with arm strength?* You hear them talk all the time about cornerbacks and their hips. *Can they play low? Can they move quickly and change directions?*

"When it comes to a kicker or a punter, though, they have no idea. So why hand out a scholarship to someone when you're not sure what it is that they do? You might as well get them to come to your school and see if they can kick. If they find a kicker in training camp, then they can give him a scholarship."

Phil wasn't finished on the topic, adding that he sees some of the same mentality in professional football. "In the NFL, there are only two teams with kicking consultants. Other than that, there is no coaching of kickers in the NFL, which is amazing. Think about it: You don't go to the NFL to get to some other higher level. This is as good as it gets, so you'd think kickers would receive a lot of coaching. But that's not the case at all.

"Now hear me out: I'm not trying to bang on coaches here. There are some special teams coaches who have learned through the years what works and doesn't work. But the facts are that NFL teams have a running backs coach, a tight ends coach, a defensive backs coach, an offensive line coach, a quarterbacks coach—all sorts of specialized coaches—but they don't have a kicking coach. Usually, that responsibility is given to the special teams coordinator. A vast majority of special teams coordinators will tell you, 'I don't mess with my kicker,' but that doesn't make sense. Yes, special teams have received increased attention in recent years, but to try to come up with a special teams game plan or philosophy without understanding the skill set of your kicker would be like trying to install an offensive system without knowing what your quarterback can do. It doesn't make sense to me."

Phil said he has a slogan when he works with coaches, and it's this: *It all starts with the kick.* "If you don't know what to expect from your kicker or what to expect from the other team's kicker, how can you possibly formulate an effective strategy?" Phil asked. "I call special teams and the kicking game the last frontier, and I think the up-and-coming coaches, the wise coaches on the fast track to promotion, would be the ones who decide to educate themselves on the kicking phases of the game. If you do that, you're going to have an advantage in one-third of the games when you get off the bus, especially in high school. If you're looking for an easy advantage, the kicking game is your opportunity."

KICKING IN BURNT ORANGE

Phil had always wanted to be a Longhorn, so when the University of Texas spun a lasso in the air, his decision to attend college in Austin was an easy one to make.

However, Phil's first year in college would prove to be a major time of spiritual testing—and a time when he made some bad decisions. "I would like to say that when I left for Texas, I was prepared to make good decisions on my own and would benefit from all the faithful contributions my parents made in my life," Phil said. "Unfortunately, I went off to school and became a knucklehead my entire freshman year of college."

Phil, who was redshirted his freshman year, wasn't playing football—which meant he had plenty of free time on his hands to socialize on Austin's famous Sixth Street and lift a brewski with his newfound drinking buddies. "I didn't realize how much of my identity had been wrapped up in my performance on the football field. When that was taken from me, I lost my way. I asked myself: *Who am I? Am I important?*"

Unbeknownst to Phil at the time, his father had reached out to the University of Texas' Fellowship of Christian Athletes rep, Reagan Lambert. Robert Dawson knew he wasn't going to have the same access to Phil once he left home, but he was willing to pass the torch of looking out for the spiritual welfare of his son to another man.

Reagan, who dropped by practice regularly, introduced himself to Phil but didn't intimate that Phil's father had called. Phil, he noticed, was pretty down and mopey since he wasn't kicking that season. Early in their conversation, Phil mentioned to Reagan that he was thinking seriously of chucking football and doing something else.

Reagan eased Phil away from the cliff, but for the rest of his redshirt year, he did his best to avoid Reagan.

"I didn't want any part of Reagan my first year at Texas," Phil said. "I was doing my own thing, all the while knowing deep down inside that I was disappointing my mother and father."

At the end of Phil's freshman year, Jerry Barlow, an FCA associate of Reagan's, invited him to an FCA summer sports camp. Phil reluctantly agreed to go, more out of love and loyalty to his parents and out of believing that saying yes to camp would make them feel better about his spiritual future. When Phil arrived at Hardin-Simmons University in Abilene, Texas, for the start of the FCA camp, staffers asked him to be a "huddle" leader, which is like being a counselor to the younger campers. Phil didn't feel worthy, but he said yes.

"I was hoping to survive the week, maybe learn a few things. But for anyone who knowingly is not living the right way, probably the last thing you want to hear is the truth of Christ and His ways. That's exactly what happened to me that week. I was completely convicted. My eyes were opened not only to the truth my parents had exposed me to, but it was time for me to take the reins, make my own decisions, and start living out what I said I believed in."

Making a turnaround wasn't easy for Phil. The start of his redshirt freshman year of football was a bit of a letdown, especially after the emotional highs of FCA summer camp. Phil was still living in his old dorm room, still surrounded by the same friends, and still trying to navigate his way around a campus with 50,000 students. Turning away from his "knucklehead" past and walking with Christ was going to take some effort.

This time around, though, Phil didn't make himself scarce whenever Reagan Lambert was in the neighborhood. The pair developed a tremendous peer-to-peer relationship that lasts to this day, despite the age difference of twenty years between the two.

"Reagan was awesome. He was patient with me," Phil said. "I'm sure he wanted to wring my neck at times, but he also knew that God's timing is always right and that sooner or later God would get my attention and help me understand these things. Certainly the answer may be different for everyone, but God was in control of everything. He let me go through some experiences to help me make up my mind to follow Him. I'm happy to say years later that the fun in life, the sweet spot in life, is experienced best when it's consistent with the fullness of Christ and His truth."

Phil won the Texas kicking job his redshirt freshman year, and he immediately made an impact. He made 14 of

15 from the 47-yard line or closer his freshman year and was celebrated as the Southwestern Conference's top kicker. His spiritual life showed progress as well: he and Reagan regularly met to go through a passage of Scripture and talk about what God was doing in their lives. He stepped up his participation in FCA events, speaking to high school and junior high students about the dangers of drugs and alcohol and about avoiding premarital sex. Reagan and Phil also prayed specifically that God would give Phil an opportunity to share his faith in a mighty way. One of Phil's prayers went like this:

God, thank You for the ability to kick a football. It's kind of a weird talent to have in this world, but that's the one You've given me, so I want to somehow use it to honor You, even if I don't understand it.

There's an old saying: Be careful what you pray for.

Within a couple of months after Phil had asked God to use him, at the end of his second year at Texas (his redshirt freshman year), Phil was suddenly presented with one of those forks in the road that continues to impact him to this day. "It is absolutely, without a doubt, the most important decision I ever made and shaped my understanding of who God is and how He works in our lives," Phil said.

Just before the start of summer school in 1995, one of Phil's coaches informed him that *Playboy* magazine had named him to its College Football All-American team and wanted to feature him in its annual September Pigskin Preview issue. All he needed to do was fly to Tucson for a series of appearances, interviews, and photo ops with Playboy bunnies and centerfolds.

"I've got to be brutally honest," Phil said. "Even though I had started tracking with the Lord, even though I was growing in my faith, and even though I was becoming more and more convinced that God's way was always the best way, when I was given this opportunity from *Playboy* magazine, my natural first reaction was 'Yes, let's do this.' "

Who wouldn't want to be recognized for being the best at what he does? In the football world, being named to the *Playboy* All-American team was a feather in your cap and a big plus with NFL scouts. Phil was only twenty years old, and this was the first time he had received the national visibility that comes with being one of the best kickers in college football.

Fortunately, Phil didn't have to say "yes" immediately. Texas head coach John Mackovic told him to go back to his dorm and sleep on it.

When Phil called Reagan Lambert to discuss the situation, he asked, "I have to turn this down, don't I?"

"I think you do," Reagan replied. "We've talked about you having influence, but we've also prayed about you having an opportunity to share your faith. This looks like that opportunity."

In the quiet of his dorm room, Phil sought the Lord's guidance on what he should do. He knew his mom and dad would never approve of him appearing in *Playboy*. Then he remembered the commitment he had made to honor God through his kicking and the conversations he'd had with Reagan about making a difference in people's lives. The decision was cut-and-dry: even though his flesh wanted to accept this award, he would say no, relying in faith that in some way God would use this situation to honor Himself.

Within a half-hour after Phil told his coach that he couldn't be part of the *Playboy* All-American team, dozens of his teammates were knocking on his dorm room door. "Are you crazy, dude?" one asked. "It's just going out to Arizona and having a few pictures taken. What's the harm?"

Several of Phil's coaches posed similar questions: "Phil, what's the deal here? You don't have to go to the Playboy mansion and get naked with the girls. It's important to be on this preseason All-American team. You're the only Longhorn to receive this honor."

Each interaction with his teammates and coaches opened the door for Phil to share his faith and tell them why it was important to him to say no. "Guys, you know me, and you know how competitive I am," he said. "I understand that it's an honor to be thought of a preseason All-American, but I can't accept this because of my faith and my position with the FCA here in Texas. I go around and talk to middle school and high school kids about putting God first in my life. I just don't think these two things line up."

After Phil told me that, we had this exchange:

You didn't know at the time that you were going to have children and someday be able to tell this story to them.

Phil: That's right because that experience was such a powerful one in my life. It keeps me accountable to this day when it comes to pornography or how I view women or raising a daughter or treating my wife. In some ways, that's an area that God has used to keep in the forefront of my daily decisions to this day.

Saying no to *Playboy* encouraged me to experience freedom and victory in the area of sexual integrity, and I know it's a tough issue for a lot of men. To now be a dad, and have two boys who are going to be drawn to the same types of things that I was certainly drawn to . . . to be able to share with them that this was my experience is very rewarding. There's a slogan I share with my kids that is a direct result of what happened with *Playboy*, and it's this: *Nine times out of ten, your feelings are wrong.*

What I'm trying to teach my children is that just because you're feeling something doesn't make it right. Chances are whatever you're feeling is the *wrong* thing to do. For instance, when someone yells at you, you feel like yelling back. A classmate cheats on a test and gets a better grade than you, and you feel like cheating so you can make a better grade than him.

In this case, you see a pretty-looking girl, and you want to look at her in the wrong way. Those feelings are natural, but even if you feel like doing that, that doesn't make it right. Whatever the issue, I want my kids to grow up knowing the truth of Scripture, which defines what's right. Feelings don't.

You see, back in 1995, my feelings were telling me, *Do Playboy. Go for it.* I was fortunate enough to be able to ignore those feelings and experience one of the greatest blessings of my life.

Was there any blowback from turning down *Playboy*?

I remember receiving a letter from the religion editor of *Playboy*.

***Playboy* has a religion editor?**

I didn't know such a person existed, but he let me have it pretty good. He said something about me being judgmental and even quoted Scripture to support his argument: "Why do you look at the speck of sawdust in your brother's eye and pay no attention to the plank in your own eye?" (Matthew 7:3, New International Version).

As a young, growing Christian, this was my first "false teaching" test. I grew up in a great home, a great church, being mentored and taught great things by Reagan, and now I had someone throwing Scripture at me and twisting its intention. I had to learn that as beneficial as it was to have good people around me, I had to study the Truth and be able to discern what is true. With the help of the Holy Spirit, of course.

Like statistics, you can bend Scripture to make it suit your purposes, and that's what the religion editor of *Playboy* magazine did. His letter forced me to pursue truth so that if I was ever presented with false teaching the next time around, I could identify it and recognize it for what it was.

Did you show Reagan the letter?

Oh, yeah, I did. He had quite a chuckle.

Following *l'affaire Playboy*, Phil's college kicking career flourished in Austin. Here are some of the highlights:

- A game-winning 50-yarder into a 20-mile-per-hour headwind to beat Virginia his sophomore year
- Being named a *Pro Football Weekly* first-team All-American his junior year
- Setting a UT record by hitting 15 straight

field goals during his junior and senior years

- Making six straight field goals from 50 or more yards
- Being named Longhorn team captain his senior year

Phil's friends and coaches were telling him that he had the leg to kick in the NFL. But NFL coaches are just as flighty as their college counterparts when it comes to drafting kickers. Many prefer to invite three or four hopefuls to training camp, toss them up into the air, and see who's still standing at the end of six weeks.

There was something else working against Phil catching on with an NFL team: there usually isn't a lot of turnover among kickers. As he heard *ad nauseum*, the NFL had room for only 30 placekickers. (The NFL would add two teams after 1999.)

THE ROAD TO CLEVELAND

Phil hosted a two-day draft party at his parents' house in Lake Highlands. He invited friends to join him for what he hoped would be his crowning moment as a football player—when NFL commissioner Paul Tagliabue would calmly stride to the podium at Madison Square Garden and announce that with such-and-such pick of the 1998 NFL draft, such-and-such team had chosen *from the University of Texas, placekicker Phil* . . .

Not surprisingly, Phil wasn't selected the first night of the draft, when rounds one and two were completed. His name wasn't called on Day 2 either, meaning his draft party was a bust. In fact, the 1998 draft was the first in twenty-five years that *no* kickers were drafted.

It seems that Dallas Cowboys president Jerry Jones had famously said that kickers were a dime a dozen and steadfastly refused to pay them much more than he did his gardener. Jones declared that he'd never draft another kicker because he could find the next one on a street corner; all he needed to do was call for an open tryout. Other NFL owners took their cue from Jerry Jones.

Okay, Phil would have to kick his way onto an NFL team.

The Oakland Raiders signed him to a free agent contact and told him to get ready to compete for a job at training camp. His main challenger was another free agent, Greg Davis, who was an eleven-year NFL veteran and a known quantity. At the end of camp, the Raiders coaching staff gave the nod to Davis. Meanwhile, Phil caught a huge break after the Raiders waived him: the New England Patriots saw enough in his abilities to assign him to their practice squad.

Using one of the eight practice squad openings for a kicker is very unusual in the NFL. But at least Phil was practicing at a top-notch facility, where he could watch and learn how Patriots kicker Adam Vinatieri—one of the best in the business—approached his job.

Phil saved money by staying at the Endzone Motor Inn in Foxboro, a motel so dreary that the only reviewer on Yelp. com said the Endzone was "one of those places where you stagger into the room, wake up the next morning, and wonder to yourself . . . why did you stay here?"

The Patriots let Phil go at the end of 1998 season, meaning his NFL aspirations were hanging by a tenterhook. The Cleveland Browns were reconstituting themselves as an expansion franchise in 1999, and they had an opening for a kicker. The Browns invited Phil to training camp, where he would be competing against two other kickers for the job.

All Phil wanted to hear was his name called—that and the news that he had won the job. The Browns' training camp, however, was a battleground that was still in doubt a few days before the season opener. With the first game of the 1999 season just days away, Phil walked into the Browns training facility and noticed head coach Chris Palmer walking in his direction.

"Phil," he said, raising a hand.

Phil's heart raced as Coach Palmer approached him. Here was the moment he had been waiting for—the moment he hoped he would learn that all the training, gym work, and practice kicks had paid off.

Coach Palmer approached Phil and stopped. "We're going to start with you," he said casually, and then hurried off to another meeting.

We're going to start with you? Phil was happy he had made the final cut, but that wasn't exactly the ringing endorsement he was hoping for. He knew what that phrase translated to in footballese: *You're our kicker for now, but if one of your kicks sails wide right to lose a game, someone else will get a shot.*

But Phil—who knows a critical miss could cost him his job at any time—hasn't just survived in the NFL for fourteen seasons and counting, he's flourished. Many say he's the best outdoor kicker in professional football. Through the 2012 season, he was the only Cleveland player to suit up every season with the "new" Browns, and the record book shows that he scored the first points for the expansion franchise back in 1999.

Over the years, Phil has quietly fashioned a résumé nearly every NFL kicker would love to attach his name to. He connected on fifteen game-winning field goals for a Cleveland team that wasn't often in a position to win games; he ranks as the tenth-most accurate field-goal kicker in NFL history (for kickers with three seasons or more under their belts); and, despite spending fourteen seasons kicking off Cleveland's chewed-up terrain half the season, he has compiled a lifetime completion average of 84 percent. Among the kickers with 300 or more field goals (there are twenty-five of them), his lifetime 84.2 percent accuracy rate ranks at No. 1.

FOCUSING ON WHAT'S REALLY IMPORTANT

Phil has worked hard to become one of the best in the NFL at what he does. But he's paid even more attention to building a strong family, which began not long after he went undrafted in 1998. While his agent worked on a free agent contract with the Oakland Raiders, Phil dropped by the Grapevine Opry, close to his hometown of Lake Highlands. His brother Peter was an aspiring country music artist and had a gig that evening at the music hall.

But someone else caught his eye that night—a beautiful singer named Shannon Sheppard. She, too, was dreaming of a career in music and had sung behind Wayne Newton for two years at his Las Vegas shows. Phil asked around for Shannon's phone number, called her, and then swept her off her feet. Their courtship was short; they were married shortly after Phil finished his season on the Patriots' practice squad. They were settling into married life when Phil claimed a tenuous grip on the Cleveland Browns' kicking position.

Meanwhile, Reagan Lambert and his wife, Debbie, made the first of many visits to Cleveland to see how the couple was doing. They reminded the Dawsons that marriage is something both partners must give 100 percent to—not the 50/50 arrangement that popular culture says it is. Two years later, their first child, Dru, was born, followed by Beau two years after that. It was the Dawsons' next pregnancy in 2006 that reminded them that NFL football, while it was his job, wasn't that important in the big picture.

Here's how Phil described what happened:

> So we're pregnant with our third and kind of got this thing down. Know how it all works. This time we're going to have a girl. That's something Shannon and I wanted. So we're kind of rolling along. The previous two children, everything went smooth and they're healthy. Life is great.
>
> Right at the end of the pregnancy, my wife came to me and said, "You know, I had my two other babies in Texas, and I feel like I need to have this baby back home." She wanted to be with the doctor who did the delivery of our two previous boys.
>
> I said if that's what you're feeling, that's what we'll do. We're getting toward the end, and Shannon flies home with the boys while I finish up the season in Ohio. When Shannon visited her old doctor, she had a sonogram. After moving the wand around, the doctor got a real concerned look on her face. Before Shannon knew it, she was in a different room with a different specialist using a more advanced sonogram machine. That's

when they lowered the boom and told Shannon that she was in pretty bad shape and so was the baby.

We had been cruising along with no signs of any trouble. We're going to have our girl, and life would be all good. We never had the idea that something could go wrong, but something *had* gone wrong. It seems the doctors had discovered a cantaloupe-sized mass growing inside her uterus. The condition was known as placenta accreta, where the placenta attaches itself too deeply into the uterine wall.

In layman's terms, that meant there was a real chance that Shannon would bleed to death when she gave birth. There was just as great of a chance that the baby wouldn't survive the trip through the birth canal. The news came as a pretty big shock. There was also the very real possibility that doctors could only save the life of Shannon *or* the baby—and I'd be forced to make some type of *Sophie's Choice*.

We didn't have a whole lot of time to let this sink in—just thirty-six hours. There were a lot of quick decisions that had to be made, and the doctors were scrambling, too. Instead of coming home and talking about what color to paint the nursery, I was reading through a sheaf of legal papers that included giving me the power of attorney able to make life-and-death decisions on behalf of my wife and my unborn daughter.

Meanwhile, the doctors were drawing up plans in the dirt, to use a football term. They came up with a two-day game plan: that afternoon, they would use an experimental procedure that involved inserting stent-like balloons in each femoral artery. Then she would have to lie flat on her back and not move for the next twenty-four hours. The following day, they would perform a Cesarean section, blowing up those balloons to stem the main blood flow to the placenta so that when the surgeons started cutting out the placenta, she wouldn't bleed to death.

Obviously, they weren't exactly sure how this was going to play out. If she was bleeding out, that would put the baby under severe stress. Her doctors also informed me that when they got into the operating room, even though they had blood transfusions ready to go and every specialist known to man in there, I had to be prepared to make a quick decision if they turned to me. If Shannon was going down, we could save only one life. Which one would it be?

Shannon was fully aware of everything the doctors were saying. She told me that if I had to make that choice, then let our daughter live. She was an angel throughout all of this. I've never seen such grace and faith.

You'd think, after turning down *Playboy* and getting a whole lot of credit for being a spiritual giant, that I would exhibit the same grace and faith. I don't know what I felt, but I know it wasn't that. I don't ever remember yelling at God, but I can tell you I got really mad. I remember really vocalizing my feelings to God. I just went into a bunker. I wouldn't let anyone help me. I didn't want to talk to anyone. I wanted to be alone. This was all happening so fast.

I remember crying out that I wanted the right answer. I knew enough to know that I wanted to do whatever God wanted, but I was getting silence in return. There was no clear *This is what you should decide.* That made me really angry.

Looking back, I can't believe how selfish I was as I was trying to process all this. I remember thinking, *Which decision would be easier on me?* I hated myself for even thinking that way. In the darkest moments, sin was revealed. I remember not necessarily doubting God, but thinking, *Really, God? You're going to do this to us?*

When Shannon encouraged me to save the baby, I even got mad at her . . . mad at her for being so eager to go to heaven and leave me to raise the child as a single-parent father. She was in total peace and almost enjoying the intimacy she was having with God, being in a situation where there was literally nothing she could do. She completely entrusted herself to her Father's care.

"How can you look forward to that so much and leave me here?" I asked Shannon. "What am I going to do?"

You could say I was feeling sorry for myself. I can remember praying that God would do His will and get me out of the way because I knew enough to know I was pretty jacked up right then.

After my wife had the balloon procedure and was in intensive care on the eve of the Cesarean section, I couldn't be with her. I sat in a hotel room at the hospital by myself, alone. And my wife was alone.

I was thinking that this is the last night on earth that I would be married and I couldn't even be with her. It was as alone and dark as I have ever felt.

I got up the next morning, and we went into the delivery room. What happened next is something none of the doctors can explain. They were absolutely floored that not only mother and baby came through just fine, but the placenta came out in one piece, which they guaranteed would not be the case. Of all the blood they had on standby, my wife didn't require one drop.

Our baby was perfectly healthy and didn't require anything. They sewed my wife up and four days later, we went home together as a family.

Seven years has passed since the birth of Sophiann, and every time I have a long moment to look at her, I remember that a miracle happened that day.

You see, I had tried to prepare myself for every available scenario, except one—that both Shannon and Sophiann would survive. I'm ashamed to admit it, but I will so people can hopefully learn from my experience. In other words, I had prepared myself for everything except God being God. That's been a very humbling experience for me.

As an athlete, I think we get way too much credit for being a Christian and having people tell me how difficult it must be to be a Christian athlete. I give speeches at a lot of different places, and if I'm not careful, I can develop a false sense of confidence about how mature I am in my faith. My experience with Shannon and Sophiann humbled me to the point where I realized, *Phil, you've got a long way to go. You didn't even once ask God to perform a miracle or consider that He could, if He chose to. You were all caught up in yourself and your own abilities.*

What happened over those two days continues to be a humbling and very revealing life experience for me.

ICING THE KICKER

After reading Phil's account of his wife's last pregnancy, you have to be impressed with his wonderful transparency. But there was another topic I really wanted to talk about before our interview ended, and it was how NFL coaches often attempt to "ice" a kicker by calling a time-out just before he attempts a game-tying or game-winning kick.

I think it's a stupid move, almost a cliché. If you're looking to psyche out the kicker, then I would think it would be better to *not* call a time-out and get into the kicker's head that way. *Will they or won't they call a time-out?* I've always thought that when a coach calls for a time-out, he's just giving the kicker more time to settle in.

My feelings on the subject were justified during one game in the 2012 NFL playoffs. The Seattle Seahawks had stormed back from way behind with 20 second-half points to take an improbable 28–27 lead against the Atlanta Falcons with 31 seconds left on the clock. Game in the bag, right?

Not when an NFL defense goes into "prevent" mode. Two long pass plays later, the Falcons were lining up for a 49-yard field goal to win the game.

So what does Seahawks coach Pete Carroll do? He waits until the last possible second to call time-out to "ice" the kicker. Just as the officials blew the whistle to stop play, the snap came out and kicker Matt Bryant thumped the kick well right of the goalposts. The home crowd in Atlanta gasped, thinking their beloved Falcons were done for the season. But the kick didn't count.

In golf terms, Bryant got a mulligan—a second chance to hit the green with his approach shot. His next kick split the uprights, and the Falcons jubilantly stormed off the field with a playoff win.

Case closed, right? Wasn't this a demonstration of how coaches don't understand kicking? I was delighted to have a chance to ask a real-life NFL kicker if he agreed.

"It would seem so," Phil said. "We stand on the sidelines for three hours to get our chance. What's another minute going to do? In the case of someone like me who plays in adverse weather conditions, being iced actually helps. Remember, I go out before the game and study the wind and the field. Over the course of the game, those conditions change. Whatever game plan I had at the opening kickoff may be actually different now. Under normal circumstances, I'm running out on the field while the 40-second play clock is running out. I have to give my spot to the holder, watch him fill it in, look at the wind, make sure I know where I'm aiming, make sure there are eleven guys on the field, see what kind of rush is coming at me . . . and then make the kick. Everything is happening real fast.

"Now you give me a time-out, and I have more time to check the field, make sure the spot is how I want it, feel the wind, make sure I know exactly where to aim, take my time counting everyone up, see what they're doing on their side, and get focused and ready. A time out allows me to be more professional at my job.

"In the old days, like with Rolf Benirschke, you'd put a lot of pressure on your kicker and see if he would crack. You just assumed he couldn't handle the pressure because he was a kicker so if he misses, the team runs, or you throw snowballs at him. But if you ask me, icing the kicker is an outdated tactic."

So there you have it, straight from the kicker's mouth. And if you're an Eagles fan and thinking of throwing a snowball in Phil's direction the next time a game at Lincoln Financial Field is on the line, forget it.

Phil Dawson will make that kick.

6

NFL QUARTERBACKS:
THE HIGHEST HIGHS AND
THE LOWEST LOWS

One afternoon, having made an appointment to speak with a player, I dropped by the San Diego Chargers practice facility. I planted myself behind the end zone and watched the offense scrimmage the defense. The action was coming toward me.

The Chargers offense wore away jerseys that were white with navy blue numbers, while the defense was clad in solid navy blue tops. On this day, the team was practicing in "shells"—NFL practice lingo for helmets, shoulder pads, and shorts.

Philip Rivers was taking reps in a relaxed atmosphere. Just another midweek practice session for him and his team-mates. The plays were starting inside the 40-yard line, around the 35-yard marker. Each offensive snap ended with Rivers either throwing the ball like a dart on short passes or with just the right amount of air on longer routes.

There was one play in regular rotation: a curl-and-go route up the right sideline. Each and every time, Philip lofted the leather ball with perfect arc for its 40-yard journey. Every throw landed softly in the sprinting receiver's cupped hands one yard inside the sidelines and about three yards from the back of the end zone.

The accuracy of each pass astounded me. Wanting to share the excitement of this virtuoso performance with someone, I made eye contact with one of the young equipment guys to my right. "Can you believe how every throw is right on the money?" I muttered.

"Yup," said one in a navy Chargers polo. "That's why quarterbacks get paid the big bucks."

There's no doubt that it takes marvelous physical gifts to stand in the pocket, peer through a plastic faceguard toward a chaotic landscape involving twenty-one moving parts, work through your progressions, and deliver a precision pass to a receiver. All this must transpire within 2.8 seconds; if not, the pocket of protection will collapse and you'll take a colossal hit from humongous defensive linemen with bad breath.

When you add in the mental toughness that every quarterback must bring to bear—the mental strength to disregard the pressures of the moment, brush off the implications of victory versus failure, and make the plays in crunch time—I say that quarterback is the toughest position in football. Maybe one of the most demanding in all of sports.

You can argue with me, but when you add the X factor of leadership to the physical and mental demands placed on quarterbacks, I can easily understand why they're the highest paid players on the team. Philip Rivers, for instance, makes around 14 percent of the Chargers payroll even though he's one of fifty-three players on the team. For the 2013 season, Rivers is being paid $12 million in base salary and a total of $17,110,00 million in compensation.

Mama, let your babies grow up to be quarterbacks.

When you add up their total compensation, a handful of quarterbacks have punctured the $20 million ceiling: Peyton Manning, Aaron Rodgers, Tom Brady, Tony Romo, and newcomer Joe Flacco, who leveraged his Super Bowl win to corral $30 million in 2013 as part of a six-year, $120 million contract. Drew Brees earns $17,400,000 in 2013, but he's due a big raise to $26,400,000 in 2015.

Crazy as it sounds, quarterbacks are worth every dollar—if they produce. But even playing well is sometimes not enough. All their superior passing skills and decision-making acumen go for naught if the team doesn't win more than it loses.

Because they're the focal point, NFL quarterbacks live with stress week-in and week-out. They hear the cheers and the boos, and deal with a fishbowl existence when in the public eye. In most games, the outcome is based upon their ability to make plays when the pressure is greatest.

It's been said that quarterbacks get all the glory in victory—and a lion's share of the blame in defeat. But think about what those magnificent wins and bitter losses mean on a personal level. Sure, winning is great, and NFL quarterbacks will tell you that regular season victories are wonderful, playoff wins are sweeter, and Super Bowl victories are over the moon. But how do they feel when the team loses?

For NFL quarterbacks, the lows of losses are much more

emotional, much tougher to get over, and last much longer than the last win. Quarterbacks will tell you that the emotional trough of losing goes much deeper than the amazing highs they experience when the confetti flies and they're showered with accolades from the media. We have no idea of the dark places a quarterback's mind will travel to after a tough loss—especially one that results from a muffed handoff, a disastrous interception, or a shocking overthrow, on fourth-and-goal, down by four points with time running out, when a receiver is open in the end zone.

During those depressing moments, I have a sense that the NFL quarterbacks who follow Christ like to park themselves and meditate on a comforting passage of Scripture. Maybe words like those of Jesus in Matthew 11:28–30 (New International Version):

> *"Come to me, all you who are weary and burdened, and I will give you rest. Take my yoke upon you and learn from me, for I am gentle and humble in heart, and you will find rest for your souls. For my yoke is easy and my burden is light."*

This is not to overly dramatize the plight of the poor NFL quarterback after a disheartening loss. Football is a game, after all, and we would all do well to remember that. NFL contests are played for our enjoyment, as a way to kick back during our leisure time. Winning may be everything to the hometown faithful, but our disposition for the week shouldn't be determined by what happened the previous Sunday. But the reality is that we as football fans are passionate, and we take our team's losses personally.

I reckon, though, that NFL quarterbacks take losses a hundred times harder. If so, quarterbacks who are looking to the Bible for emotional support during adverse times deal better with the pain of losing, the accountability they face from their coaches, and all the other stuff happening *off* the field—the online criticism in the blogosphere, the snarky columns in the newspaper, and the pointless pontifications from the postgame pundits.

Just as I can't imagine going through life without my personal relationship with Christ, I can't see how quarterbacks can handle all that adversity without the Lord to get them through the low moments.

But what do I know? I've never played quarterback or coached football, so I asked my old friend Mike Riley—head coach of the Chargers in the early 2000s and now coach at Oregon State—for his thoughts.

Mike was a standout quarterback at Corvallis High in Corvallis, Oregon, and led his team to the state championship. The University of Alabama recruited him but turned him into a defensive back. Whatever his position, he was playing under the legendary Bear Bryant.

Mike started coaching soon after college, working his way up to the offensive coordinator's job at the University of Southern California. In his first college head-coaching job—at Oregon State in the late 1990s—Mike quickly turned around a program that had been a Pacific Northwest punching bag for decades.

That success caught the eye of Bobby Beathard, the San Diego Chargers' general manager, who offered Mike a job in the NFL. After three tough seasons as head coach of the Chargers—known as the "Ryan Leaf years" in San Diego—and one season as an assistant at New Orleans, Mike returned in 2003 to Oregon State, where he's regularly exceeded expectations. Though Mike and his coaching staff have to turn over rocks to find prospects overlooked by other teams, the Beavers have had some great nine-win seasons.

For nearly forty years, Mike has watched hundreds of young quarterbacks play the position. He looks for more than ability—their athleticism, size, speed, and arm strength. What Mike really wants to see is leadership. He's searching for smart, charismatic men who can gain the respect and confidence of their teammates.

Great quarterbacks perform well in stressful situations and are willing to sacrifice for the team. They understand that the game is not only about them. The good quarterback's mindset has to be: *How can I make this team successful? Because if we're successful, I'm going to be successful.*

Here's what Mike Riley had to say in our discussion:

Coaches are in the business of evaluating players. What were you looking for during quarterback tryouts?

Mike Riley: I have a lot of admiration for quarterbacks because it takes tremendous courage, intelligence, and ability to play the position. I've seen all kinds over the years. I've coached 5-foot, 8-inch Doug Flutie and 6-foot, 6-inch Derek Anderson and everything in between. They were all good, and they were all different.

There are a lot of intangibles that go into quarterbacking,

and everyone wants to know what they are. Sometimes we sum it all up and say, "He's got *it*—the 'it factor.' " When a quarterback walks on the field, you want to be able to point to him and say, "That's our quarterback right there."

I think the ability to have things appear slow to you so that you have good vision on what's going on when everything else is moving so fast is super important. Some guys get so overwhelmed by the speed that they don't see anything.

Vision is so important. Some guys can't describe anything that's going on out there. They might have the arm and all the ability in the world, but they can't see anything. I also believe everything goes back to the word *poise*—when a quarterback is cool, calm, collected, and yet competitive. I think you have to combine all those attributes.

How do quarterbacks show leadership?

Mike Riley: There is a fine line in quarterbacking between "I'm going to do this, make this throw" and doing something dumb and forcing the football. They have to be able to say to themselves, *I can't do this at this time, so I'm not going to make this throw.*

Quarterbacks have to keep their wits about them but at the same time they have to have that competitive nature. The other thing involved in that "it factor" is physical toughness. They have to look right down the barrel of getting hit. They know they are going to get hit, but their eyes have to be downfield where they are throwing the football.

No human being is naturally good at that. If somebody is going to hit you in the mouth, you're probably looking out for it. Quarterbacks have to have incredible toughness. They have to throw with pinpoint accuracy. And it all has to be done in a split second.

What have you seen that's different in quarterbacks who take their Christian faith seriously?

Mike Riley: If things aren't going good, which happens to every quarterback, I've seen their Christian background help them get through those tough times better.

Perspective is really important at the quarterback position. I think it's important in any sport. A quarterback who is a Christian has an opportunity, through his faith, to have a good perspective. He knows that there is going to be good and bad and has to maintain a stability and consistency. I think Christianity can give us a stabilizer in life, something we can always go back to.

There is something bigger than the sixty minutes in the game. When the crowd is booing and everything is falling apart, it helps that they know God loves them. They can always have that stability in life, which is a very important part of our faith.

There's a misunderstanding about Christianity in some areas and it goes like this: *If you're a Christian, you're not a tough guy.* I've found that to be absolutely untrue. We've been given the advice in Scripture that whatever we do, we're to do it heartily for Him. To me, if you're playing football and doing it heartily for the Lord, if you're doing it the way the game is supposed to be played, then you're playing in a tough, physical fashion.

If you're going to be a good quarterback, if you're going

to win, then you have to put in the time. I think everywhere in the Bible there are lessons about remaining steadfast and not overcome with worry. Those two things are big deals for a quarterback.

ROLL CALL

I've done the best head count I can, and I would say there are a good thirty-five starting and backup NFL quarterbacks—out of eighty-five or so in the league—whose Christian faith underpins their existence. That's a high percentage, more than 40 percent, which begs these questions: Why are there so many Christian quarterbacks in the NFL? Is there something about the position that draws young men who are followers of Christ?

I've thought about what the best answer should be. Sure, the case can be made that teams will get behind a quarterback who demonstrates servant leadership, a phrase coined back in 1970 by Robert K. Greenleaf in *The Servant As Leader*. The servant-leader puts the needs of others first and helps those around him develop and perform as highly as possible—which, in the NFL world—would help the team win. When the team wins, the quarterback is successful, which completes the circle.

While the foundation of servant-leadership is certainly biblically based (Matthew 20:27–28 says ". . . and whoever wants to be first must be your slave, just as the Son of Man did not come to be served, but to serve . . ."), Robert Greenleaf never mentioned Christ or quoted from Scripture in his groundbreaking essay.

Looking back through fifty years of NFL history, it

appears that the most successful quarterbacks were the ones who felt—or were taught—that they could best lead the team by getting out in front and having their teammates follow in their steps. But teams also respond to quarterbacks who are servant leaders, and they do that by taking the blame when things go wrong. You never see good quarterbacks pointing the finger at a receiver when he drops a pass. After a tough loss, they're the ones telling the media, "It was my fault. That one's on me. I should have done better."

When something goes right and the team scores a big victory, team-first quarterbacks hand out a lot of accolades to their linemen and receivers and thank the coaches for making the right play calls. They talk about how everyone played so well. They use their platform to praise their teammates.

From my seat in the grandstands, I can see the benefits of being a Christian while trying to quarterback a team. You need to stay humble, work with your teammates to get the best out of them, encourage them to never give up, and rely on God. You don't have to be a Christian to do the first three of those things, but I would think that understanding that God has a plan for your life and that you should trust in Him for the outcome, whatever it is, would put you in the best frame of mind to succeed at the quarterback position.

So let's celebrate the quarterbacks I'm featuring in this NFL edition of *Playing with Purpose*. I'll first talk about the Three QBs from my first *Playing with Purpose* book—Sam Bradford, Colt McCoy, and Tim Tebow—and then follow (in alphabetical order) with features on other NFL quarterbacks whose faith is important for them, whose core values are Christ-centered, and whose strength of character comes from knowing that there's something more to life than being an NFL quarterback, no matter how highly esteemed they're held in today's culture.

THE THREE QBS: SAM BRADFORD, COLT MCCOY, AND TIM TEBOW

During the spring of 2010, my literary agent, Greg Johnson, called with an intriguing idea: Why not write a book on three Christian quarterbacks entering the NFL that season—Sam Bradford, Colt McCoy, and Tim Tebow?

These three young men wore their faith on their jersey sleeves and spoke boldly about Christ. Not only that, they were *really* good quarterbacks. Sam, forgoing his senior year at the University of Oklahoma, was projected to become a No. 1 draft pick. Colt was a highly regarded quarterback coming out of the University of Texas who had suffered a nasty shoulder injury in his final collegiate game, the BCS National Championship game against Alabama. Tim Tebow, was, well, Tim Tebow—the most talked-about quarterback on the planet, college or pro.

So how have things turned out for the Three QBs?

I'd say that their status going into the 2013 season is probably not what they imagined it would be when they entered the NFL three years earlier—full of hope and optimism for the future. Maybe Sam Bradford, who's experienced middling results as the starting quarterback for the St. Louis Rams, feels things are on track for him. But Colt McCoy and Tim Tebow have endured more twists and turns in their first three seasons in the NFL than the Matterhorn bobsled ride.

We'll start, though, with Sam Bradford.

✷ ✷ ✷

Sam Bradford was hailed as the savior of the St. Louis Rams when the franchise drafted him No. 1 in 2010. Coming off a glittery three seasons at Oklahoma, he checked all the boxes: tall at 6 feet, 4 inches, off-the-chart passing accuracy, quick decision-maker, and good character.

Raised as a single child by godly parents Kent and Martha Bradford, Sam was a sports prodigy growing up in Oklahoma City, Oklahoma. Put a ball or stick in his hands, and his tremendous hand-eye coordination bloomed like a spring rose. His parents ran themselves ragged getting Sam to all his football, basketball, baseball, and hockey games.

Football was Sam's first love. There was something about orchestrating an offense down the field with all eyes on him that flipped on his competitive juices. A college star at the University of Oklahoma, he was a Heisman Trophy winner who won a lot of games for the Sooners. Sam skipped his senior year to turn pro and signed the biggest rookie contract ever: a six-year, $78 million pact that included $50 million in guarantees.

Sam had a very good rookie year, taking the Rams to the brink of the playoffs with a 7–9 record. (A win against the Seattle Seahawks in the season's final game would have done it.) Sam was accorded Rookie of the Year honors, and everyone felt the Rams were on the right track. Sam's sophomore season in the NFL was one he'd like to forget, though. A high ankle sprain kept him out of six games. When he was playing, Sam regressed, but so did the team—big time. A 2–14 record meant that the

2011 Rams shared the title of worst team in the NFL with the Indianapolis Colts.

The Colts got the first pick in the 2012 draft and announced beforehand that they were going with Stanford's Andrew Luck. That meant Robert Griffin III was next up on the big board. But the Rams had Sam, so they were in good position to demand a heavy price to pry away their No. 2 pick. The Redskins mortgaged their future to take Robert Griffin III.

Sam and the Rams bounced back with a 7–8–1 record in 2012, laying a foundation for the future, to be sure, but they missed the playoffs. Sam's fans are waiting for him to *dominate* opponents—blowing their doors down with breathtaking passing—but that hasn't happened yet.

So the 2013 season looks to be a pivotal season for Sam. Head coach Jeff Fisher, in his second year with St. Louis, has some good draft picks to work with. Sam will also be in his second year with a new offensive system. A fortified offensive line and an upgrade or two in the receiving corps will help.

★ ★ ★

When the Cleveland Browns first signed Colt McCoy, after choosing him in the third round of the 2010 NFL draft, they told him that rookie quarterbacks watch the game from the sidelines with a clipboard in hand, so he could forget about playing his first year.

Then the two quarterbacks ahead of him went down, and the third-stringer got his chance. Colt's first NFL start was in Pittsburgh, a lion's den for road teams. Colt played well and showed uncommon poise against the Steel Curtain defense. One start begat another, and Colt seemed to be making the statement that he was the Browns' quarterback for the future.

Unfortunately, the entire Browns' coaching staff was fired after a second-straight 5–11 season, and a new regime, with Pat Shurmur at the helm, came on board. Colt still looked poised to start at quarterback in Cleveland, but the NFL was in the midst of a "work stoppage"—meaning no official off-season practice sessions. Colt, hoping to improve his team's offensive play in 2011, hosted his first "Camp Colt" in Austin. Browns players flew in from around the country for three days of player-run drills and practice.

The NFL and the players association eventually reached an agreement, ending the work lockout. The Browns got off to a promising 2–1 start, but soon the losses piled up like snow drifts. Cleveland finished 4–12 in 2011, and Colt missed the final three games of the season after taking a vicious helmet-to-helmet hit from Pittsburgh linebacker James Harrison in Week 14.

Fast forward a few months to the 2012 NFL draft. Shurmur and his staff are under the gun following the 2011 failure. It soon became evident that the Browns were in the process of greasing the skids for the end of the Colt McCoy era in Cleveland.

First, general manager Tom Heckert whispered out loud that he was shopping Colt to other teams. Then the Browns selected quarterback Brandon Weeden, a former New York Yankee farm team player who resurrected his football career at Oklahoma State, with the 22nd pick in the first round of the NFL draft. Weeden was twenty-eight years old, making him the oldest first-round draft pick in NFL history.

Colt was no longer the Browns' starting quarterback, not with the coaching staff so heavily invested in Weeden. Colt wasn't allowed to compete for his old job in training camp; the coaches handed the keys to Weeden and did their best to prepare him to play in the NFL.

Having established himself as the team leader the previous two seasons, how was Colt supposed to handle the demotion? It wasn't in his nature to act pouty, and he knew it wouldn't be fair to Weeden or his teammates if he made known his disappointment. Colt played the role of good teammate and kept his mouth shut while Weeden tried to find his footing. The Browns finished 5–11 in 2012, and Colt played just 39 snaps in three games late in the season when Weeden went down with an injury. New owner Jimmy Haslam fired Shurmur (and Heckert) and installed Rob Chudzinski, formerly offensive coordinator at Carolina, as head coach.

As the deck was being reshuffled, Colt caught a break—in my opinion. The new coaching regime traded Colt to the San Francisco 49ers during the off-season, where he'll be in a supporting role to Colin Kaepernick, who came out of nowhere to lead the 49ers to the Super Bowl during the 2012 season.

Colt said he has no hard feelings for what happened in Cleveland and would always be grateful for his time with the Browns. He knows that God has a plan for his life, whatever that will be, and this is part of the journey.

So we'll have to sit back and see how everything plays out in San Francisco. In the meantime, Colt's a smart young man who came up with a wonderful word picture for quarterbacking that goes like this:

Be the river, not the flood.

Here's how that saying works. If you're a river, then you're staying in your banks. You're flowing in the right direction. Your current is powerful enough to carry ships—or a team. Your team moves with the flow.

But when you're a flood, your waters spill beyond the banks and run rampant through the countryside, causing havoc and destruction. There's no control. That's why when you're a quarterback, you want to be the river, not the flood.

Maybe Colt will get his chance to be a river again.

TIM TEBOW

It's Father's Day 2012, and I'm sitting with 26,000 sun-baked San Diegans bunched on one side of Qualcomm Stadium. We're looking toward a large stage in the west end zone, where a tight worship band leads the "congregation" in praise songs sung in English and Spanish.

We're all here for one reason: to see Tim Tebow in the flesh. When Shadow Mountain Community Church in nearby El Cajon announced that Tim would be in the house on Father's Day, demand for seating was so great that the service was moved to a football stadium—a *big* NFL stadium.

That's how it is with Tim Tebow. Of the Three QBs, none has been written about, talked about, scrutinized, debated, and dissected more than Tim, the former Heisman Trophy winner at the University of Florida and the surprise first-round pick of the Denver Broncos in the 2010 NFL draft.

Tim has his share of detractors but *more* than his share of adoring fans—as I witnessed up close in that 2012 Father's Day service in San Diego. That day, thousands of people showed up, not to see him play football but to hear what he had to say.

He's certainly never been shy when it comes to talking about his faith in Jesus Christ, and he sees his NFL career as a platform from which he can point others toward Him.

As for Tim's NFL career itself, it certainly has been a rollercoaster ride. His stardust 2011 season, when he grabbed the reins of the Denver Broncos and spurred them to the playoffs and an improbable win over Pittsburgh, was a study in contrasts. Tim won ugly, won playing beautifully, and won improvising—but he won.

The biggest thing Tim had going for himself *and* for the Broncos—since it's always about the team for him—was that he had that special ability to raise the level of his game when it counted most. *Winning time* is something that can't be taught. Some players have that talent, many don't. In Denver, Tim proved that he is a winner with an uncanny ability to yank victory from the jaws of defeat.

Although the Denver Broncos spurned Tim for Peyton Manning prior to the 2012 season and shipped him to the New York Jets (*Thanks for taking us to the playoffs, Tim!*), many of Tim's fans—and Tim himself—believed God wanted him playing in the nation's media capital for a reason.

I know what a lot of Tim's fans *wanted* to happen in New York during the 2012 season: Mark Sanchez, the embattled Jets starting quarterback, would flounder early in the season, and cries of "Tebow! Tebow!" would fill MetLife Stadium in the Meadowlands until an exasperated Rex Ryan tapped Tim on the shoulder and told him to go in and win the game.

He'd done it before in Denver. Now he'd show Gotham what Tebowmania was *really* about.

Except he never got a chance to put his winning ways on

display. Sure, early in the season, Ryan inserted Tim into the lineup on third-and-short running situations, but those opportunities dwindled as the Jets' dismal season progressed. Then the Jet coaches made Tim a member of the punt team, giving him the job of *blocking* for the punter as his "personal protector." That's the equivalent of sending a thoroughbred into the field as a plow horse.

Even when Sanchez went down late in the season with an injury, Ryan looked past Tim and went with an untested rookie, Greg McElroy. When the Jets' 6–10 season was in the books, stories surfaced that Tim's days in the Big Apple were over.

The Jets kept Tim until the NFL draft, and then after tabbing West Virginia quarterback Geno Smith, the die was cast. Tim was released, presumably because no team wanted to trade for him. As the 2013 season was taking shape, Tim was scrambling outside the pocket again—this time for his football life.

No team appeared to want him until the New England Patriots took a flyer on Tim to play behind Tom Brady and backup Ryan Mallett. The move reunites Tim with Patriots offensive coordinator Josh McDaniels, who was Denver's head coach when the Broncos traded into the first round to take Tim in the 2010 draft.

So why is Tim Tebow's career as an NFL quarterback hanging by a leather football lace?

It must be that loopy hitch in his throwing motion. All too often, he drops his left hand down to waist level before starting an elongated swoop of his left arm prior to releasing the ball. NFL coaches like to see their quarterbacks holding the ball at chest level so they can get the ball out of their hands sooner. How soon? Tim's throwing motion takes .60 seconds to complete, where the average NFL quarterback needs .40 seconds. In the NFL, a split second is often the difference between a completion and taking a sack—or a cornerback breaking up a pass play.

I understand that what worked for Tim at the high school and college level—the longer throwing motion—doesn't cut it in the NFL. But even with his unorthodox throwing motion, when Tim has been given time in the pocket, he has shown flashes of brilliance as a passer.

I'm rooting for Tim to find consistent success as an NFL quarterback. I think the guy is a miracle worker who finds a way to win, and he's obviously a man of amazing faith, unblemished character, and resolute integrity. But the tale of Tim Tebow is a sober reminder that it takes more than terrific intangibles and sheer determination to be successful in the Not For Long league—you also must possess elite passing skills.

You can rest assured, though, that no matter what God has in store for Tim Tebow, he'll use whatever platform the Lord gives him to bring glory to Jesus Christ.

DREW BREES

I live a few miles—and a few million dollars in real estate value, as the locals say—from Del Mar, California, a trendy beach community where a handful of NFL quarterbacks have purchased homes for their off-season enjoyment. Aaron Rodgers and Carson Palmer maintain residences in Del Mar, as does Drew Brees, the New Orleans Saints' starting quarterback.

I've been impressed with Drew ever since my wife and I met him and his wife, Brittany, during his rookie year in San

Diego, when they were seated at our table during a Huntington's disease fundraising dinner. He was personable, chatty, and made eye contact when he talked with us.

A second-round pick in the 2001 NFL draft, Drew had some great years in San Diego, but in 2004 the Chargers drafted a 6-foot, 5-inch passing wizard named Philip Rivers, who couldn't sit on the bench forever. After all, San Diego had given up the draft rights to Eli Manning to get this kid, and he had waited two seasons for a shot.

But Drew was playing too well to come off the field. Then, in the last game of the 2005 regular season against Denver, Drew fumbled a snap on his own goal line. The ball squirted onto the ground and sat there like an unprotected Easter egg. Instinct took over, and Drew dove for the ball a split-second before 325-pound Broncos' tackle Gerard Warren pulverized his right shoulder. When Drew stood up, his right elbow was suddenly up high—like he was starting the "Funky Chicken" dance and had to stop. His elbow was at a weird angle because his shoulder had been gruesomely dislocated.

Seven years and counting since Drew's injury, it's difficult for people to remember just how mangled his throwing shoulder was from the mash-up with Warren. Dr. James Andrews, the sports orthopedic surgeon from Birmingham, Alabama, doubted that Drew would ever be able to comb his hair without pain, let alone return to the NFL as an elite passer.

The Chargers front office could read the medical reports as well as anyone else, and they made a low-ball offer for Drew to return to the team, which was the same as a vote of no confidence. It looked as though they wanted to start the Philip Rivers era in San Diego.

Drew explored his options and found a team that had been kicked to the curb—just like him. That team was the New Orleans Saints, one year post-Hurricane Katrina. The Saints were wandering migrants during the 2005 season, forced to play "home games" in Tigers Stadium in Baton Rouge, Louisiana, the Alamodome in San Antonio, Texas, and Giants Stadium in New Jersey because the Superdome needed an overhaul after becoming a hellhole of a residence for tens of thousands of desperate NOLA residents during and after Hurricane Katrina.

When Drew arrived in New Orleans to be wooed by the Saints, head coach Sean Payton drove him through some of the city's ravaged neighborhoods. As Drew witnessed the devastation up close—the boarded-up and battered homes rotting away—Payton told him, "Just as you're rebuilding your career, you can help a city rebuild."

"I'm very faith-driven in my life," Drew said. "At some point in the process I started to believe that maybe God put me in this position for a reason. Maybe we were supposed to come to New Orleans and do more than just play football."

That is exactly how it played out for Drew and his family.

Drew's all-world passing skills helped turn a struggling franchise into a playoff team that advanced to Super Bowl XLIV during the 2009 season, which went a long way toward restoring the city's fragile psyche. Remember, we're talking about an area that had been slammed by a monster hurricane that destroyed 70,000 homes and flooded 85 percent of the Crescent City.

Now Drew and his teammates had a chance to give their hungry fans something to cheer about. During the Saints' up-and-down forty-three-year history, the team had never been to a Super Bowl, and not that much time had passed since New Orleans fans wore brown paper bags over their heads and called their home team "the Aints."

Now their fans hoisted homemade signs that read, "Who dat?"—shorthand for "Who dat say dey gonna beat dem Saints?"

The Hurricane Katrina storyline going into Super Bowl XLIV is part of why 111,300,000 viewers tuned in to watch the game on TV. But football fans also found the matchup between Drew and Peyton Manning of the Indianapolis Colts intriguing. Many observers believed it was possible that whoever had the ball in his hands on the last possession would decide the game.

The second half was a We-Score-They-Score scenario. Drew and the Saints forged a 24–17 fourth-quarter lead, but Peyton Manning had plenty of time to lead his team down the field and send the game into overtime. The Colts were driving deep into Saints territory when the unexpected happened: Saints defensive back Tracy Porter jumped a route on Manning for a pick-six. Suddenly, what had been a close, tense game was in the Saints win column—31–17.

Drew has so much talent that he could throw a football— with a Hollywood assist—through his neighbors' windows. He's on pace to become the one of the greatest NFL passers ever and, at the start of the 2013 season, already has several milestones in his possession, including:

• most passing yards in a single season (5,476, set in 2011)

• highest completion percentage in a season (71.2 percent, also set in 2011)

• most consecutive games with at least one touchdown pass (54, set in 2012 and breaking Johnny Unitas' record)

There are a several other Drew Brees achievements I could cite, but his greatest off-the-field legacy will be the work of Drew and Brittany's Brees Dream Foundation, which has helped with revitalization projects in New Orleans, among other worthwhile charitable endeavors.

KIRK COUSINS

The Washington Redskins drafted two quarterbacks in the 2012 NFL draft, a highly unusual move for any NFL team. Of course, if you're a quarterback hoping to be drafted into the NFL and it's the fourth round and your name hasn't been called yet, you're still thrilled when Commissioner Roger Goodell calls your name—even when the quarterback your team took ahead of you happens to be Heisman Trophy winner Robert Griffin III.

That was the situation Kirk Cousins walked into when he showed up for the Redskins' 2012 training camp. Even though he was given zero chance of beating out Griffin for the starting spot, he performed admirably and beat out incumbent starter Rex Grossman for the backup job.

If you're any kind of NFL fan, you probably know that Kirk had to come in and relieve the injured RG3 during some pressure-packed moments leading to Washington's return to the playoffs in 2012. In the playoff loss to the Seattle Seahawks—the one in which Robert Griffin III wrecked his left knee—I was raising my voice at coach Mike Shanahan to yank RG3 off the field (because he could barely move) and get Kirk in there and let him be the hero.

Kirk has been underestimated most of his life, starting back in sixth grade, when he played tackle football for the first time. After tryouts, a youth coach relegated him to the B team, which he promptly led to the league championship.

Kirk grew up as a PK—a preacher's kid. His father, Don, was one of the first pastors Bill Hybels hired when he founded Willow Creek Community Church—one of the first megachurches in the country—in suburban Chicago in the mid-1970s. Don and his wife, MaryAnn, received the scare of a lifetime when nineteen-month-old Kirk reached for a boiling pot of spaghetti on the stove. The scalding water spilled onto the toddler, severely burning his upper torso. Kirk screamed to the high heavens, and his parents raced in. When they took his clothes off, they discovered that the scalding water had removed a layer of skin from his neck, shoulders, chest, and abdomen. Fortunately, the boiling water didn't fall on his head, or the accident might have killed him.

Don and MaryAnn rushed Kirk to the emergency room, where things were touch and go for several days. His temperature spiked to 106 degrees, putting him close to death. Doctors administered burn treatments, and Kirk spent nearly two weeks recovering in the hospital. For the next year, he wore a special jacket that compressed his skin. The young boy made a full recovery and went on to become a talented athlete who competed in youth baseball, basketball, and football.

Before Kirk started high school, his family moved to Holland, Michigan, where his father launched his own ministry coaching Christian leaders within churches and parachurch organizations. Kirk played quarterback at Holland Christian School, which competed in the Class B division in Michigan. Kirk was an outstanding high school quarterback, but a broken ankle his junior year slowed down the recruiting train.

Only a pair of Division I FBS schools recruited him—Toledo and Western Michigan. Kirk was deciding which scholarship offer to take when the Michigan State coaches called at the last minute, saying they'd like to offer him a scholarship . . . *if* one of their more highly regarded quarterback recruits turned them down.

So if you're willing to wait a bit . . .

And that's how Kirk ended up at East Lansing. Kirk had to overcome all sorts of hurdles, but he led the Spartans to a pair of eleven-game winning seasons and three huge victories over Big Blue—Michigan.

I first heard about Kirk just prior to his senior year at Michigan State in 2011. He had given such a vigorous and passionate speech that it went viral and was forwarded to hundreds of thousands, if not millions, via the Internet.

The venue was the Big Ten Kickoff Luncheon before the 2011 season. I watched his seven-minute speech, and he knocked my socks off with his podium presence and vocal delivery. Here are a couple of snippets:

• "And it's here, in this place of privilege, where perhaps danger lies. I have been taught that human nature is such that the 'place of privilege' most often and most naturally leads to a sense of entitlement . . . the notion that I deserve to be treated as special, because I am privileged.

"The truth is privilege should never lead to entitlement. I've been raised and taught to believe that privilege should lead to responsibility; in fact, to greater responsibility. The Bible says in Luke 12:48: 'From everyone who has been given much, much will be demanded; and from the one who has been entrusted with much, much more will be asked.' "

- "We have a responsibility to use the platform we've been given to provide a true example of what it means to be a young man to those ten- and twelve-year-old boys who see us as bigger than life. I know this to be true, because just a few short years ago, I was one of those twelve-year-old boys . . . and I remember well how I looked up to the players whose position, by God's grace, I'm standing in today."

- "We could redefine what is 'cool' for young people. We could set a new standard for how to treat others. We could embody what it means to be a person of integrity. We could show young people that excellence in the classroom is a worthy pursuit. We could show that it's more important to do what *is* right, than to do what *feels* right.

"While I believe we as players, do not deserve the platform we have been given . . . we have it nonetheless. It comes with the territory of being a college football player in the Big Ten. May we as players have the wisdom to handle this privilege and the courage to fulfill the responsibility we've been given."

Maybe Kirk should stay in Washington, D.C., when his football career is over. We could use leaders like him in the halls of Congress.

COLIN KAEPERNICK

The biggest story during the 2012 NFL season?

For the regular season, it was the play of Robert Griffin III. For the NFL playoffs, it was the ascent of Colin Kaepernick, the tattoo-festooned quarterback of the San Francisco 49ers.

Man, did he become *large*. Had he and 49ers cashed in on

a first-and-goal from the 7-yard line late in the fourth quarter at Super Bowl XLVII, it's likely that he'd be the toast of the NFL going into the 2013 season.

Colin is a fascinating talent. He brings to the field a lethal combination of size (he's 6 feet, 4 inches tall), blazing speed, a howitzer for an arm, and an ability to improvise. Players use a single word to describe the kind of sensational physical talent Colin possesses: *sick*.

If you followed the 2012 season, then you know that Colin got his chance to take over as 49ers quarterback when starter Alex Smith went down with a concussion in Week 10. Colin was very sharp in leading the 49ers to key wins over Chicago and New Orleans, but it was the *way* that Colin played that set head coach Jim Harbaugh's heart fluttering like a schoolgirl's. There was the quickness to avoid a sack, the live-wire arm and ability to throw into tight windows, the explosive speed when the pocket broke down, and the panache in his play.

This from a kid who was two seasons removed from the University of Nevada (Reno), not actually a "cradle for quarterbacks" like Purdue or USC.

When Smith, who had missed two weeks with his concussion, was cleared to play, he returned to the 49ers' locker room fully expecting to have his job back. After all, in his last full game before his injury, against Arizona, he went 18-for-19 passing and was named the NFC's Offensive Player of the Week. Besides, there's an unwritten rule in the NFL: You can't lose your job because of injury.

Scratch that unwritten rule. Harbaugh kept Colin as his starter, saying he was going with the quarterback who had the "hot hand." Smith took the demotion as you might expect: "It sucks," he said. "I don't know what else to say."

Meanwhile, Colin played like a house on fire. But surely he couldn't handle NFL playoff pressure, not with a thin résumé of seven career starts. The responsibility would be too great, the pressure too intense.

He certainly looked overwhelmed in the first quarter of the 49ers' NFC Divisional playoff game against Green Bay. On the game's first series, he telegraphed a short pass on a down-and-out pattern, and Packers cornerback Sam Shields jumped the route for a 52-yard pick-six.

On the next series, Colin was missing on short pass plays and faced a third-and-10 on the 49er 33-yard line. After the snap, he was chased out of the pocket, looked like he might run the ball, then, while he was on the run, lobbed a rainbow pass to Frank Gore.

The 45-yard gain changed everything. I noticed Colin's body language after the big completion; he reacted like forty-pound shoulder pads had been removed. Three plays later, he tucked the ball and sprinted untouched to the end zone from 20 yards out, and San Francisco never looked back, winning 45–31.

When the 49ers advanced to Super Bowl XLVII, Colin became the feel-good story of the playoffs. We heard and read about how he had been adopted by Rick and Teresa Kaepernick, who were looking into the adoption option after their two infant sons died from congenital heart defects shortly after birth. The Kaepernicks were already parents of another son and daughter.

On the other side of the equation, Heidi Zabransky was a 6-foot, 2-inch star athlete growing up in Brookfield, Wisconsin, who became pregnant when she was eighteen. The father, who has never been identified, was also 6 feet, 2 inches tall.

Give the young woman credit: she chose life for the un-born child growing within her. Her parents stood behind her during this crisis pregnancy. Early on, Heidi thought she would raise the child herself. But then a friend who worked for the Lutheran Social Services in Wisconsin talked to her about adoption. Heidi interviewed three couples, but none clicked until she met the Kaepernicks and agreed to "place" her child with the family.

Imagine the emotions this young mother felt after giving birth. According to Wisconsin law at the time, the Kaepernicks could not have the child until six weeks had passed since birth. Usually, the child would go into foster care for that interim period, but Heidi kept the infant with her. Bonds naturally form between a mother and her infant son, and as Heidi cared for and suckled Colin during those six weeks, her mothering instincts kicked in. The hardest day in Heidi's life had to be when she handed over young Colin to the adoption officials, who carried the boy to another room and another life with the Kaepernicks.

Heidi eventually married, taking the last name of Russo. Now a dental nurse and the mother of a young son, Heidi created a kerfuffle during the run-up to the Super Bowl when, during an interview with a Denver TV station, she said she had tried to contact Colin for four years but that he'd declined to see her in person or speak with her on the phone.

At the Super Bowl media day, ESPN columnist Rick Reilly asked Colin why he felt that way and if he thought it would it be disrespectful to his parents to meet with his birthmother.

"No," Colin said. "It's not really a respect thing. It's just . . . that's my family. That's it."

"But aren't you curious?"

"No."

The Kaepernick parents told Reilly that they would have no problem with Colin speaking to Heidi, but he wasn't ready yet. He didn't want to be seen as being disloyal to the only parents he has known.

Colin was raised in a Christian home, so it's easy to imagine that he has prayed about this difficult situation. He's been talking about his faith in Christ since long before celebrityhood landed in his lap in San Francisco. He's also talked about what those tattoos on his arms, chest, and back mean.

The tattoos that adorn Colin's arms are more than skin deep. They are a series of Bible verses:

• Psalm 27:3 (left bicep): "Though an army besiege me, my heart will not fear; though war break out against me, even then I will be confident."

• Psalm 18:39 (right bicep): "You armed me with strength for battle; you humbled my adversaries before me."

Then there are the two hands clasped in prayer with the words "to God the glory" below Psalm 18:39. That's the tattoo that Colin kisses in celebration whenever he runs for a touchdown. Colin has the most ink on his back, where he has images of angels and demons battling to win the line of scrimmage in a good-versus-evil motif.

Just as I'll never understand rap music, I'll never get tattoos, which aficionados call "body art." I guess it's the permanency of tattoos on the skin that bothers me. Football players seem to forget that life changes—and fashions—go in and out of style. For twenty-five-year-olds looking at an average life expectancy of seventy-eight years, that's more than half a century with the same old tattoo in the same old place, its message getting lighter and lighter on wrinkling skin as every year goes by.

Can you have a tattoo and still be a Christian? Of course you can. And it's nice that Colin has chosen Bible verses and themes as his tats. Young kids look up to that.

At the same time, though, I can't get comedian Sebastian Maniscalco's recent line out of my mind:

"Why would you put a bumper sticker on a Ferrari?"

CHRISTIAN PONDER

Minnesota Vikings quarterback Christian Ponder has quite a love story to tell. In October 2012, he met Samantha Steele on the set of ESPN College GameDay, where the attractive blonde hosted the first hour prior to picking up her sideline reporter duties later that day.

Talk about love at first sight. Just two months later—a week before Christmas, while the Minnesota Vikings were in the midst of a playoff run—Christian and Samantha eloped.

Vikings fans were slack-jawed. A key player getting married in-season with just two games left on the schedule? What was the rush? Hadn't they just announced their engagement two weeks earlier, when Christian arranged Christmas lights across the deck of his home so that they spelled out *Marry me.* (I guess Christian was in too much of a hurry to make the proposal in the form of a question—or he ran out of lights.)

On the late afternoon of Monday, December 17, 2012, the giddy couple slipped across the Wisconsin/Minnesota border and were hitched inside St. Croix County Court in Hudson, a half-hour east of downtown Minneapolis. A court commissioner pronounced them husband and wife. No family or friends were present.

"We tried to keep the attention away from us and went over to Wisconsin and had it done," Christian told reporters after word leaked out about the nuptials two days later. "So it was quick but it was good."

This wasn't a late-season bye week, so Christian had practice the next day in preparation for an important road game against the Houston Texans. At least they had their wedding night.

Christian's teammates ribbed him pretty good, calling him "Mr. Steele." And after Christian had a great game the following Sunday in a win in Houston, Vikings coach Leslie Frazier planted his tongue firmly in cheek and told reporters that Christian "should get married more often."

Christian said it was important that they get married before the holidays for "a lot of personal reasons" and that they'd have a big celebration when the season was over.

From what I've read, Christian and Samantha are both solid Christians. Samantha attended Liberty University in Lynchburg, Virginia, the largest Christian university in the world. She was the daughter of a coach and played volleyball, softball, tennis, track, and basketball growing up in Phoenix. Her Twitter feed says "God first, people second, cake third. Jeremiah 17:7."

Christian, the middle of three boys, grew up in Colleyville, Texas, which is located not far from Dallas. His father, David Ponder, had played on the defensive line at Florida State and played one season with the Dallas Cowboys.

David could be tough on his son. One time, after Christian left the house ten minutes late for an 8 a.m. throwing session with his receivers, his father reminded him that the difference between mediocrity and greatness could be those ten minutes. David and his wife, Christine, provided their boys a Christian home and did their best to instill godly values and discipline. David was pleased when Christian decided to follow in his footsteps and play his college ball at Florida State. Though he battled numerous injuries, Christian had a fine college career for the Seminoles.

Christian took his academics seriously, entering college with advanced placement, graduating in two-and-a-half years with a finance degree, going for his MBA, and then collecting his second graduate degree, in sports management.

One of Christian's career highlights at FSU was being awarded the Bobby Bowden Award his senior year at a Fellowship of Christian Athletes breakfast before the BCS National Championship game. The Bowden Award, named after the former Seminole coach who had mentored Christian's father, is presented annually to the college football player who best conducts himself as a "faith model" in the community.

The Vikings took Christian with the twelfth overall pick in the 2011 NFL draft, which was good timing for him because Brett Favre, Minnesota's starting quarterback in 2009 and 2010, had retired for the third and final time. Christian's rookie year, however, was a learning curve. He and his Vikings teammates struggled to a 3–13 record.

But what a turnaround in 2012. Christian and the Vikings showed great improvement, beating Green Bay at home in the season's final game to finish 10–6 and qualify for the playoffs. Unfortunately for the Vikings, they had to play the Packers again six days later in Green Bay—this time without Christian, who had to miss the game with a nasty elbow injury he had suffered at the tail end of the regular season win over the Packers.

When the 2012 season was over, the newlyweds began making plans to . . . get married all over again. In April, Christian and Samantha did it up right before family and a few hundred of their closest friends in Samantha's hometown of Phoenix.

Call me traditional, but what I love about their marriage is that Samantha now identifies herself as Samantha Ponder on ESPN broadcasts.

I think that's really cool.

PHILIP RIVERS

When the San Diego Chargers play at home, I sometimes ask my mom if she saw Philip Rivers at the 7:30 a.m. Sunday Mass.

"Yup, Philip was there," Mom will invariably say.

"Did you say hello?"

My mother then gives me one of those *Are you kidding?* looks.

"Of course not," I say for her. But I'm glad to hear that Mom and other parishioners give Philip a wide berth on Game Day. Professional athletes should be able to worship in peace.

Philip is a Roman Catholic who takes his Christian faith seriously and has spoken at youth church events like Ignite the Truth. He was also a presenter at the "Strong Men, Strong Faith" men's conference, held at Good Shepherd Catholic Church in Huntsville, Alabama. He's outspoken about abstinence before marriage and tells youth groups that he remained chaste until he and his wife, Tiffany, were married when they were college students.

Philip leads the NFL in one category that has never received much attention but should be shouted from the rooftops: the number of children with one wife. He and Tiffany are the proud parents of six children, so let any NFL married couple top that. (Unfortunately, some players have sired more children out of wedlock with multiple partners.)

As you can probably tell by now, I'm a San Diego Chargers fan, having grown up living and dying with the team's fortunes. I'm also a Philip Rivers fan and regard him as belonging among the top tier of NFL quarterbacks. Although the Chargers haven't qualified for the playoffs the past couple of years, I believe that once Philip gets some decent blocking and a bigger running threat, his arm will shred NFL defenses like it has in the past. He's just thirty-one years old, so he's not at the tail end of his career yet.

I've interviewed Philip a few times, and two things struck me: his energy and his size (he towers over me at 6 feet, 5 inches tall and has muscleman biceps that could break me in half). He's got a lot on his plate: running the Chargers offense, dealing with the media as the face of the Chargers franchise, balancing the demands of being a dad to six children he dotes on at home, and pouring any leftover energy into his charitable endeavors. He's a pro's pro who's in the Charger's training facility by 6:30 every morning during the season and constantly works out in the offseason.

He told me two stories that were classics. The first was about what happened at his first minicamp after San Diego traded for him after the 2004 NFL draft. The team was hosting an OTA—Organized Team Activity—and Philip was running a few plays in which he was checking down his receivers. When he saw no one was open, he threw the ball away. This happened several times.

Later that day in the film room, Philip watched the practice session on tape, and his offensive coordinator at the time, Cam Cameron, paused the film. "See that?" he said, pointing to the receiver with a red dot of light. "He's wide open."

Philip did a double take. *That guy was wide open?* he thought. *He was covered like a blanket.*

And then a realization came over him. In college, Philip's open receivers often got good separation from defensive backs and were easy to find. But in the pros, there was *almost always* tight coverage. He had a split second to get rid of the ball, and he had to throw it *very* accurately into tighter windows.

Philip had to be on time because the time his receiver was open until the time he was covered was over just like that—a snap of his fingers. If Philip threw the ball a hair late, his pass would be intercepted. He found that out when his very first throw in team practice was picked and run back for a touchdown, which led him to another revelation as a rookie: *When they pick it off, they usually score with it.*

The other story concerned the adjustments Philip had to make when he was approached for autographs out in public. He had heard that Green Bay Packers legend Bart Starr always treated his fans with respect, even when they approached him while he was having dinner at a restaurant. Starr said he did that because he knew it would probably be the only time that the fan would ever meet him in person, and he never knew what kind of impact his courtesy would have on that person.

During the 2008 season, the Chargers lost to the Atlanta Falcons at home to fall to 4–8. Philip had never lost so many games at any level, and he was really feeling down. He took his time showering and getting dressed before going to face the media. He then glumly walked out to the players' parking lot to his car. He slowed down just before he exited the Qualcomm Stadium parking lot, thinking, *We're four-and-eight. I can't believe it.*

To his right, Philip spotted a ten-year-old boy standing next to his mom and holding a homemade sign that said, *Can I have your autograph?* Not feeling especially sociable, Philip stepped on the gas and blew right by him. Then he looked in his rearview mirror and saw a dejected boy hang his head as his mother tried to console him.

A pang of guilt stabbed Philip's conscience. The Chargers QB immediately flipped a U-turn in the middle of the road. He sped back into the Qualcomm parking lot, drove up to the mother and son, and rolled down the window. "Hey, I'll sign," he said, and they came running over. Philip will never know what that gesture meant to the young boy, but on a day when the boy's favorite team suffered through an especially brutal loss, it was probably just what he needed to lift his spirits.

Philip's heart is bent toward helping young kids realize their dreams, which is why he and Tiffany support charities that help unwanted, abandoned, and orphaned children find "forever families." He has used some of his time and money to help recruit adoptive families and then provide them with financial aid and assistance so that they're in a better place to adopt foster kids and orphans.

Philip understands that there are thousands of children in San Diego's foster care system and that resources are limited. That's why it's important to him and to Tiffany that they do all they can to help place needy children in a loving home, to buy them things like cleats or musical instruments, or to give them birthday gifts on their special day.

Philip said his eyes were opened to the plight of foster kids when he met two sisters who told him and Tiffany that whenever their social worker dropped by their foster home, it meant one thing: time to pack their bags. They were moving on to the next home and their next foster parents.

Philip's low-key charitable efforts helped place kids like these two sisters into permanent homes with mothers and fathers who pledge to love and raise them—and give them hope for the future.

Sounds to me like Philip is putting some legs on Jeremiah 29:11—and like he is passing along his devout faith.

TONY ROMO

I've seen Tony Romo play several times—on the golf course.

Tony comes to San Diego every spring to tee off in a celebrity tournament that draws a lot of NFL players. He's quite a stick, the best "pro athlete" golfer in the country. He's got a plus-3 handicap, which means that he's expected to be three shots under par when he plays a round. Back in 2011, he reached the sectional qualifying stage for the U.S. Open.

You may be wondering why I've included Tony in this

group. Wasn't he the guy who dated a lot of starlets and famously spent a weekend in Cabo San Lucas with singer/actress Jessica Simpson in 2008, when the Cowboys had a first-round bye in the NFL playoffs?

Yes, that's all true. But what most people don't know is that Jessica's parents accompanied the couple and that there were other "chaperones" on the trip, including Cowboys tight end (and strong Christian) Jason Witten with his wife, Michelle, plus several other Cowboys players and their significant others. Whatever happened in Cabo, I have a feeling that having his love life featured on the pages of *People* left Tony wanting.

A few months after breaking up with Jessica Simpson in 2009, Tony started dating Candice Crawford, a former Miss Missouri. They married in 2011 and have a son named Crawford, who was born in 2012.

It's evident that Tony has settled down and gotten more serious about his faith in recent years. He participated in a men's conference sponsored by Prestonwood Baptist in Dallas and sat down for an interview afterward with Dr. Jack Graham, Prestonwood Baptist's pastor, who asked how he was handling such a high-profile position as quarterback of "America's Team," the Dallas Cowboys.

"How has your faith helped you do that?" Graham asked.

"I can easily pinpoint one time that stands out to me and allowed me to have the right perspective, I guess," Tony answered. "It was my second year in the NFL, and we had Quincy Carter coming back at quarterback. Coach Bill Parcells had brought in Vinny Testaverde to challenge him for the position.

"The first couple of practices, I struggled because I was pressing. I knew I had to do something special. I remember about the third night in training camp having this easiness come over me as I was praying. I gave it all up to the Lord.

"I said, 'If I'm meant to be assistant club golf professional back in Burlington, Wisconsin, I'm okay with that.' As I gave it up to the Lord at the time, it freed me up to go out and throw the football. Let it go. If I throw it five yards over the receiver's head, it goes five yards over his head. But I'm going to throw hard, and I'm going to stay after practice, be there before, and see what happens. I knew it wasn't all about me.

"That was a neat thing that happened that day, and today, when I get into tough moments, I go right back to that and say, 'It's all part of His plan.' "

The Burlington, Wisconsin, that Tony mentioned is his hometown. What he didn't say was that there were *four* quarterbacks invited to training camp his rookie year and that the Cowboys were only going to keep three.

The fact that Tony was even putting on a Cowboys jersey was amazing since he was an undrafted free agent out of Eastern Illinois, a Division I-AA school. But he hung on by his fingernails and continued to work hard in practice. Two years later, during the 2006 season, he got his chance to start at quarterback in the NFL.

The 2013 season will be Tony's eighth as the Cowboys' starting quarterback. But, as he told Dr. Graham, being the spiritual leader in his home is his most important role these days. "My greatest success is when I walk that spiritual journey and when I'm that spiritual leader of my family. That's what I'm striving for and that's where I hope to continue to grow," he said.

MATT RYAN

He's the quarterback no one ever talks about—at least outside of Atlanta.

Matt Ryan is a guy who quietly goes about his business—and who has quickly earned the respect of his peers around the NFL. One player I interviewed for *Playing with Purpose* crinkled his eyebrows when Matt's name came up. "He's scary good," said the player.

In 2012, Matt piloted his team to an NFC-best 13–3 regular season record and came within a game of taking the Atlanta Falcons to the Super Bowl. He's as unflappable as a third-grade teacher on the first day of school. He was given the nickname "Matty Ice" as a teenager because he performed so well under pressure at William Penn Charter School in Philadelphia.

Late in the 2012 season, Matt talked about his faith at an FCA outreach event at the First Baptist Church of Douglasville in suburban Atlanta. When he was asked about how his faith intersects with sports, he had this answer: "They're completely interwoven. People ask me all the time, 'How do you separate what's going on at home with what you're doing on the football field?' and the honest answer that any player would tell you is, 'We don't.' Things that go on in your house or things that go on in your faith affect the way you show up to play and what you do on the field. . . . God gives you those talents for a reason, so make them count."

Then Matt was asked if he ever closed his eyes during a game and whispered one of those quick *Oh, Lord, please help me* prayers.

Matt smiled. "In all honesty, I've never found myself doing

that during a game. *Before* games, though, it's a different story. One of my favorite things about Sundays is our group prayer together. We've got people from all different types of backgrounds, all different kinds of upbringings, all different dimensions of faith, too, but everyone is together. Everybody is working toward the same goal. It's one of those things that give me comfort when I go out there, relaxed and trusting the ability I've been given."

NFL opponents are hoping Matt doesn't get any more relaxed. He and the Falcons are tough enough to beat as it is.

MICHAEL VICK

During the summer of 2012, I was asked to read the final galleys of *Finally Free*, the autobiography of NFL quarterback Michael Vick, both to give the manuscript a final proofing and to render my professional opinion of how the confessional book played out.

Even many non-football fans know who Michael Vick is—the guy whose conviction for running a dog-fighting operation turned him from an NFL star into a celebrity convict hated by animal lovers across America. Few football players have risen to such heights of NFL popularity only to fall to the depths of pubic disdain that a prison cell can bring.

One story at the beginning of the book was telling. Michael began by describing how he didn't have an easy childhood growing up in the projects, where drug dealing, drive-by shootings, and other serious crimes were the norm. His grandmother introduced him to the Christian faith and took him to the Solid Rock Church in his hometown of Newport News, Virginia. When he was fifteen years old, he started sleeping with a Bible under his pillow—as a way to stay close to God and to have a feeling of protection.

When Michael became a football star and started hanging out with the wrong people, he all but forgot his introduction to Christ. As the No. 1 overall pick in the 2001 draft, Michael came into the NFL with the Atlanta Falcons amid great fanfare. He soon demonstrated that he was the prototype of the mobile quarterback who could hurt you with his arm or with his legs. Overnight success filled his coffers with tens of millions of dollars—in salary and endorsement income—and also had him swimming in a pool of celebrity.

He also swam with the sharks—a posse of assorted friends and hangers-on who lived in houses he owned and relied on him to pay the bills. I won't re-create how he got into dog-fighting—a "sport" he said was part of the culture where he grew up—but it wasn't pretty.

When Michael was implicated in a dog-fighting ring in 2007, the media treated him as the worst of the worst kind of criminal. He was carved up in the court of public opinion and fed to the wolves. A different court—a federal one—sentenced him to two years in prison for his involvement in the Bad Newz Kennels dog-fighting ring. Making things worse for him, the Falcons won a $20 million reimbursement from his $37 million signing bonus.

There's something about losing your freedom and being behind bars that changes your focus. Michael had plenty of time to think about what had gotten him there, how he had written his own rules to life, and how he believed he was bulletproof.

There was only one person he could turn to—Jesus Christ,

and he was reminded of that when Tony Dungy, a godly man who had had a successful NFL coaching career before joining NBC as a commentator, visited him in his federal prison cell in Leavenworth, Kansas. Dungy mentored Michael and worked with him to restore his walk with God. Pastors from prison ministries reached out and ministered to him, too.

I was impressed with the arc of Michael's story in *Finally Free* and believe his contrition is real. He acknowledged his mistakes, served his time, and asked for forgiveness. He also started reading his Bible again—and God's Word once more found a place under his pillow.

Michael served nineteen months in prison before returning to the NFL in 2009. He was broke and broken, and many said he shouldn't be allowed to play in the NFL again. Fox News contributor Tucker Carlson even said the canine killings, maimings, and torture he sanctioned and even encouraged were so heartless that he deserved to be executed.

I thought that was ridiculous. God hates our sins just as much as He hated what Michael did. Besides, as Jesus pointed out to a group of religious leaders who wanted to execute a woman they'd caught in the act of adultery, who are we to cast the first stone?

So I've forgiven Michael Vick, and I hope the rest of America does, too. Sure, his best days are behind him and his 2012 season with the Philadelphia Eagles was a bust. But he's only thirty-three years old and certainly capable of surprising us with greatness again.

I don't think God is done with Michael yet, just as He's not done with any of us.

RUSSELL WILSON

With a few breaks—and a bit of timely defense—Russell Wilson and his Seattle Seahawks could have played the San Francisco 49ers in the 2012 NFC Championship Game for the right to go to Super Bowl XLVII. But when the Seahawks' eight-man secondary collapsed in Atlanta, the greatest fourth-quarter comeback in NFL playoff history—a three-touchdown rally that Russell had orchestrated—went *pffft*.

Think about the storyline *if* Seattle had advanced to the NFC title game. The media would have gone nuts about the matchup between Russell Wilson and Colin Kaepernick—two rookies who came out of nowhere to become NFL stars, two dual-threat quarterbacks who, like Robert Griffin III, gave defenses fits with the read-option, and two godly young men who weren't into the late-night party scene.

If you think Colin Kaepernick has an unlikely-to-make-it-in-the-NFL story, wait until you read about Russell Wilson.

Russell didn't play at an overlooked school like the University of Nevada, but he did have a bigger black mark against him coming out of North Carolina State and the University of Wisconsin: he was under six feet tall. (I'll explain why he played at both colleges in a minute.) Some say that he has to get on his tippy toes a bit to even reach his listed height of five feet, eleven inches, but that's immaterial. He's clearly under six feet tall and looks up to Drew Brees, who's glad to give up the honorific title of Shortest Quarterback in the NFL.

NFL scouts and coaches have an institutional bias against passers who are under 6 feet, *2 inches*, let alone six feet. They like their quarterbacks to stand tall in the pocket and survey the secondary like feudal lords without having their vision blocked by Jolly Green Giants like 6-foot, 6-inch Jared Allen. They like taller quarterbacks because they have an easier time getting their throws *over* the outstretched arms coming their way.

No one was giving Russell much of a chance to make an impact when he arrived at the Seahawks minicamp shortly after the 2012 NFL draft, when he was taken in the third round. But three days in May and 400 throws later, head coach Pete Carroll knew that Russell was going to push past incumbent Tarvaris Jackson, a five-year veteran, and Matt Flynn, a free agent who had been languishing in Green Bay behind Aaron Rodgers, for the starting job in training camp. The conventional wisdom was that since Seattle had plunked down $10 million in guaranteed money to bring Flynn into the fold, it was his job to lose.

The quarterback competition in Seattle wasn't even close. Russell so outplayed his rivals that Pete Carroll didn't equivocate. He had his quarterback, even if he was shorter than every other starting quarterback in the NFL, even if he was a rookie, and even if the Seahawks got nothing for the $10 million they invested in Matt Flynn. Russell Wilson was his guy.

"More than anything, I think they [the Seattle coaching staff] saw how I prepared," Russell said just before the start of the season. "I've been the same way throughout my whole life just because of the way my parents raised me by focusing on the little details, the attention to detail."

Those details are reflected in how his father, Harrison III, insisted that young Russell lock eyes when he was introduced to an adult and shook a hand. When he walked, feet were to be lifted, not shuffled. Homework had to handed in on time. Later on, his father said if Russell was in any type of business situation, then he needed to be dressed in a coat and tie. That's why Russell is always well attired for his postgame press conferences. When he appears in public, he looks like he just stepped off the pages of *GQ*: handsome, clean-cut, and polished like the Hope Diamond.

Russell's the product of great genes and hands-on parents, Harrison III and Tammy Wilson, who raised him and his older brother Harrison IV—everyone called him Harry—and younger sister, Anna. The family set down roots in Richmond, Virginia, where Dad was a successful lawyer, giving the family the means to send Russell and his siblings to an expensive private school called Collegiate School from kindergarten through their senior years. Russell meshed well with other students and buckled down in the classroom to reap the benefits of an elite education that cost his parents an astronomical $20,000 a year.

Harrison III knew firsthand how important academics *and* athletics could be. A baseball talent, he also excelled playing wideout in high school football in Jackson, Mississippi, an experience he used as a springboard to get into an Ivy League school—Dartmouth College. Harrison was one of those rare two-sport collegiate athletes on the Dartmouth campus in New Hampshire, playing baseball and football.

Harrison was good enough that the San Diego Chargers drafted him as a receiver in 1980, but he was the last man cut in the final week of training camp. Actually, this was probably a blessing in disguise because he took his LSAT and got into the University of Virginia law school, where he earned his degree and met his wife, Tammy, a UV undergraduate.

Harrison taught both his sons how to play baseball and

football, and taught them well. Harry was six years older than Russell, which made basketball games in the driveway tough sledding for the younger brother. But Harry loved catching passes from Russell when they played football in the backyard, and when Russell got older, his father would drive the two boys to the University of Richmond to work on their pass-and-catch drills. In the spring, Dad would pitch batting practice and hit ground balls to improve the boys' baseball skills.

In high school, Russell was clearly good enough in either sport to go on to the collegiate level. But college recruiters—like their NFL brethren—didn't like the fact that he wanted to play quarterback but wasn't at least six feet tall. "We think Russell would make a great defensive back," they all said.

North Carolina State, though, wanted Russell to come to Raleigh to play quarterback on the football team *and* to play baseball. That's a tough double in Division I, but he was up to the task. After football season was over, Russell would wake up at the crack of dawn every day to lift, go to class, and then play baseball in the afternoon.

During his redshirt freshman year, when Russell was splitting time behind center with two other quarterbacks, his father suffered a diabetes-related stroke and appeared to be brain dead. Doctors prepared the family for the worst. If he did survive, they said, he would likely be left in a vegetative state. But not only did Harrison come out of a coma, he walked out of the hospital and was able to see Harry get married.

Watching his father struggle to get back on his feet wasn't easy for Russell, who had a lot on his plate at NC State. He claimed the starting quarterback spot his sophomore season and continued playing very well for the Wolfpack baseball team in the spring—so well that on June 8, 2010, the Colorado Rockies drafted him in the fourth round of the Major League Baseball draft.

Then his father died the following day. He was fifty-five years old.

Russell mourned the loss of his father and ached to ask his advice about what he should he do. Should he cash in his football chips and try baseball? Or should he show everyone that, despite his average height, he could be a great quarterback?

Russell decided to plant cleats in both camps. He returned for his junior year at NC State in 2010 and had a great season, leading the Wolfpack to a 9–4 record, including a bowl win against West Virginia. Then he told Tom O'Brien, his football coach, that he was going to report to the Rockies' spring training camp and see how things turned out in the baseball world.

O'Brien wasn't on board, especially after Russell missed spring practice to play for the Rockies' Class A team in Asheville, North Carolina. Coach and player agreed that it would be best if they went their separate ways.

But Russell had an ace up his uniform sleeve. Since he had already graduated from college, he had the option of transferring and playing at another Division I school in the fall of 2011. In addition, the grass looked a lot greener on a football field after he batted just .228 in 61 games for the Asheville Tourists. Inquiries were made, and the University of Wisconsin said they'd love to have him.

Nice timing. Russell won the starting quarterback job in training camp, led the Badgers to the Rose Bowl, and then told the Rockies he was putting baseball on hold while he tried to make it in the NFL.

I'd say Russell Wilson has closed the deal; not only can this guy play like gangbusters, but he's also shown the hidebound NFL that you don't have to have basketball height to be a topflight NFL quarterback.

RUSSELL WILSON: SHARING GOD'S WORD ON TWITTER

I have a feeling that Scripture memorization, as well as knowing the Bible, were big deals in the Wilson household when Russell was growing up. I say that because Russell is quite the Twitter guy, and his daily tweets include a Bible verse for that day. A couple of samples from his official Twitter account:

• "Behold the proud, His soul is not upright in him; but the just shall live by his faith" (Habakkuk 2:4, New King James Version)

• "My soul, wait silently for God alone, for my expectation is from Him" (Psalm 62:5, New King James Version)

7

GREG SCHIANO:
COACHING WITH PURPOSE

Greg Schiano is the Tampa Bay Buccaneers head coach who's molded, cajoled, shouted, and blown his whistle at hundreds of football players over the years. His uncompromising pursuit of excellence motivates him to mold young men into better football players and better persons.

Greg is a rigid, discipline-minded coach whose gap-toothed grin reflects the great delight he takes in pushing his players to their physical limits. There's no sloughing off when you're on Greg Schiano's practice field. You're not allowed to put your hands on your hips or bend over at the waist when you finish a set of station-to-station drills. That shows fatigue, and you don't let the other team know you're tired. You buck up and move on to the next drill, remaining cool, calm, and collected, trying not to even breathe hard.

But Schiano, who has the reputation of being the most

physically demanding coach in the NFL, is anything but an aloof disciplinarian. He demands the best from himself before he demands the best from you, and if you give it to him, he's got your back.

I learned this about Schiano when I got to know one of his former players, a young man named Eric LeGrand. I had the privilege of collaborating with Eric on his autobiography *Believe: My Faith and the Tackle That Changed My Life*, which was released during the 2012 football season.

Perhaps you recognize the name. Eric LeGrand played football at Rutgers University from 2008–10. He was a defensive lineman and a fierce special teams player who was part of the Scarlet Knights' "bomb squad" on kickoff coverage. An exuberant sort who could be counted on to blow up kickoff returns, Eric loved to knock down blockers like bowling pins and plant the kick returner deep in his own territory.

Eric's life changed in very profound ways on October 16, 2010, when Rutgers hosted Army at the Meadowlands, the home of the New York Giants and New York Jets. The Scarlet Knights had just scored a touchdown to tie the game 17–17 with just five minutes to go in the fourth quarter.

Eric, standing at 6 feet, 2 inches tall and weighing 275 pounds, was built like a slag heap. He stretched his trunk-like legs and took his position on the kickoff team next to Rutgers' kicker, San San Te.

Te lofted the ball into the crisp autumn air, and Eric broke into a sprint. He filled his lane and looked for a pair of blockers to double-team him. Eric's sterling reputation on kickoff coverage preceded him, but this time he made a quick move to his left and slipped past a mini-wedge of blockers. Suddenly, there was open space in front of him. Malcolm Brown, the Army kick returner, was rapidly coming in his direction.

I've got a clean shot, Eric thought. His eyes and mind quickly calibrated what he needed to do to slam his shoulder into Brown's chest—and perhaps dislodge the football. Then, in the flicker of a moment, just before Eric was about to pop Brown, one of his Rutgers teammates dove for Brown's legs, causing the Black Knight return man to twist his body. Instead of driving his shoulder into the runner's midsection, Eric speared the back of Brown's left shoulder with his helmet—a bone-crunching collision audible even to those sitting in the nosebleed seats.

Two of Eric's neck vertebrae, the C3 and C4, snapped upon impact. He stiffened and slammed to the ground, landing on his back like a mighty oak that had been felled in a single chop. The injury caused the nerve stem between Eric's brain and the rest of his body to go haywire, and he struggled just to breathe.

Two Rutgers trainers immediately sprinted onto the field. Running in close pursuit was Greg Schiano, the Rutgers head coach who'd recruited Eric. The entire way, Coach Schiano shot arrow prayers into the heavens: *Lord, please don't let this be. Please let Eric be okay.*

As the Rutgers trainers assessed the situation, Coach Schiano got down on his knees and leaned into Eric's view. "Eric, you've just got to pray," he said. "Just pray that you're going to be fine."

But his player wasn't going to be fine. In fact, Eric was completely paralyzed from the neck down, unable to move his arms, torso, or legs. That's why he was fighting to gasp air into his lungs. Panic was written all over Eric's face.

While emergency personnel did their best to stabilize Eric, Schiano told an aide to find his mother, Karen LeGrand, and bring her onto the field. She wouldn't be too hard to find in the parents' section: she always wore a scarlet Rutgers jersey with Eric's number 52 on the front and back and LEGRAND'S MOM emblazoned across the back of her shoulders.

When Karen arrived on the scene, Coach placed both arms on her shoulders and locked his eyes onto hers. "Just pray," he said. "Just pray."

Karen's heart was in her throat as she watched her son being strapped to the backboard and then carted to an ambulance waiting on the side of the field. She hopped in for the drive to Hackensack University Medical Center in Hackensack, New Jersey, about five miles away.

Meanwhile, there was a game to finish, which Rutgers won, 23–20. Coach Schiano was duty bound to speak to the media afterward, and his knuckles were white from gripping the podium so tightly. With a clenched jaw, he looked out at the assembled reporters and delivered this statement: "Let me start with Eric LeGrand. He has been taken to Hackensack Medical Center. If I could ask you—and I know it's your job—but if we could respect his family and his privacy right now, it would mean a lot to me and his family. As soon as it is appropriate, I will get word to you. I promise.

"It's all tough stuff. When you coach these kids, they're your kids. That's the thing I don't know if everyone gets. It's not pro football. Those are your kids. You're raising them and finishing the job of the parents, so it's tough."

Then Schiano excused himself and rushed to the hospital in

Hackensack, where he walked into a waiting room crowded with Eric's extended family and friends. With a cell phone glued to his ear, he feverishly worked his contacts, asking if they knew of a better hospital for Eric, or if there was a top-notch neurosurgeon or specialist who could be consulted.

Long after midnight, Schiano collapsed into an uncomfortable chair. He was awakened at dawn when the lead neurosurgeon came out of the operating bay following eight hours of delicate surgery on Eric. He overheard the surgeon explain to Karen that the reason the operation had taken so long was that screws had to be set into Eric's upper spinal cord to keep it straight, which was paramount in his ability to swallow in the future.

Swallow? What about walking? Coach Schiano comforted Karen, who couldn't fathom that her son was fighting just to keep breathing and swallowing.

Amid the heavy gloom, the neurosurgeon added that with spinal cord injuries, the first seventy-two hours were crucial. He explained that if Eric was going to make some sort of recovery, then he needed to show movement during that time frame.

Schiano got his first look at Eric on Sunday evening, when he was allowed to visit the heavily sedated young man in the intensive care unit. The coach searched Eric's droopy eyes and reminded him that he loved him and would be there for him in the difficult days ahead.

Eric pushed through the haze and attempted to speak. "Coach . . . do you think I can play in the NFL?"

The out-of-left-field question hit the coach like a slap to the helmet, but he kept his teetering emotions in check.

"Your chances are as good as anyone else's," he said, hoping that Eric wouldn't see the tears pooling in his eyes.

Schiano went home late Sunday evening. Monday marked the start of another week of football practice. After the last coaches' meeting ended, around 10 p.m., he departed the Rutgers' practice facility for the Hackensack University Medical Center, arriving at the ICU around 11 o'clock. After doing his best to buoy the spirits of Eric's exhausted family members and friends, Schiano sidled up to Eric and told him that his teammates and coaches couldn't stop talking about him in the locker room and that Scarlet Nation was praying for his recovery. Schiano stayed for two or three hours before returning home to Piscataway for a couple of hours of sleep.

Meanwhile, the seventy-two-hour yardstick passed, and Eric was still unable to move any part of his body below his neck. The neurosurgeon in charge of Eric's care confirmed to Karen the horrible news that everyone feared: Eric's fracture of the C3 and C4 vertebrae was so high on his spinal column that he had a 0 to 5 percent chance of regaining neurologic function. In other words, his chances of walking or moving his arms again were practically nil.

Throughout Eric's first week at Hackensack, Schiano would arrive every evening around 11 p.m. and stay for a few hours, checking on his player and comforting family and friends in the hallway. Exhaustion set in, and there were times when he fell asleep in a chair with a computer on his lap. Video of the next opponent's offensive and defensive tendencies continued looping in the background.

During the second week after Eric's injury, Coach Schiano could no longer maintain the pace of daily late-night visits, but he phoned every day to check on Eric's progress. As Schiano told the media, one of his sons had gone down, and he wasn't going to abandon him. For the rest of their lives, Eric LeGrand and Greg Schiano would be joined.

In a statement to the media, Schiano said, "We're going to believe that Eric LeGrand is going to walk onto that field with us. That's what we will believe."

I liked how Coach Schiano used the word *believe*, which became a motto for Eric and is the reason we named our book *Believe*, which is much more than just the tragic saga of a twenty-year-old football player cut down on a field and consigned to a motorized wheelchair for the rest of his life, barring a miraculous recovery. If you've read *Believe*, then you understand that the emotional thread woven throughout the book is the heartwarming relationship between a young African-American football player and a white football coach twenty-five years his senior.

UP THE COACHING LADDER

Greg Schiano—pronounced *Shee-ah-no*—is a New Jersey native who grew up in Wyckoff and went on to Bucknell University in Lewisburg, Pennsylvania, where he was a star linebacker and voted the team's most valuable player. He graduated with a business degree and had his eye on attending law school. In 1988, while he was preparing for his LSAT test, he kept himself busy as an assistant coach at Ramapo High School, where he had played for Coach Mike Miello.

Miello was amazed at what he saw in his young assistant. "I came home the first day of double sessions and told my wife, 'Guess what? This kid is never going to see a day of law school.' He's out there like he's been there twenty years. He's a natural."

Clearly catching the coaching bug, Schiano did forsake law school. In 1989, he served as a graduate assistant for the Rutgers football team, performing mundane duties like prepping the scout team or driving coaches around on recruiting trips. But his year at Rutgers opened the door to receiving the same graduate assistant position at Penn State in 1990. That position turned into his first real coaching assignment, as a defensive backfield coach.

Having Joe Paterno's program on your résumé—at least in the early 1990s, long before the Jerry Sandusky scandal—opened doors in the football world, so when the Chicago Bears began looking for a defensive assistant in 1996, Schiano got the job. At the age of thirty, married and with a child on the way, Greg Schiano's coaching future was on a rising trajectory.

But there was just one piece missing in Schiano's life—a relationship with Christ and the hope of eternal life beyond this temporary existence on earth.

Around this time, the Bears' director of college scouting, Mike McCartney, and his father Bill, the head coach at the University of Colorado and the founder of the Christian men's organization known as Promise Keepers, spoke at a prayer breakfast. One day, Mike McCartney handed Greg a cassette tape of their talk and encouraged him to listen.

The only time Schiano had a few minutes to pop the tape into a cassette player was on his drive home from the Bears' practice facility. What he heard impacted him deeply because he could relate to Bill McCartney's story about the negative effects football had on family life. He listened intently as the Colorado coach described how he learned what was really important—having a personal relationship with Jesus Christ.

Schiano said he had to listen to McCartney's talk several times to get his message through his helmet-like skull, but one evening on his way home, he unmistakably heard God's call on his life. He pulled over to the side of the road, bowed his head, and repeated Coach McCartney's invitation to receive Christ.

As Greg's spiritual life took root and grew, he and his wife, Christy, would become parents of four children. On the football front, at the start of the 2001 season, Schiano accepted his first head coaching position—at Rutgers University. He had come full circle: a New Jerseyite returning to the place he'd gotten his first assistant college coaching position.

Rutgers was known as the "Birthplace of College Football" because the first-ever intercollegiate football game was played on the muddy plot of land where the university's gymnasium stands today. On November 6, 1869—just four years after the end of the Civil War—the Rutgers eleven took on a contingent from Princeton in a game that resembled rugby more than football. They must have had different scoring back then, too, because Rutgers won 6–4. (I'm sure the result wasn't two field goals besting two safeties.)

But Rutgers in the early '00s was far from a glamour football coaching job. By the time Coach Schiano arrived, the Rutgers football team hadn't finished a season with a .500 record for more than a decade. That may have been one reason he kept his job even after the Scarlet Knights posted 2–9, 1–11, 5–7, and 4–7 records during his first four years at

Piscataway. It was during Schiano's fourth season, in 2004, that his path first crossed that of Eric LeGrand, a freshman middle linebacker at Colonia High School, near Eric's hometown of Avenel, New Jersey.

Eric had started the season on the JV team, but when injuries cast the varsity middle linebacker to the sidelines, he was called up for the last three games. He made the most of his opportunity. The freshman linebacker was all over the field, a defensive maniac who made fifteen tackles his first game, seventeen the next, and thirteen in the final game of the season.

Colonia High was only twenty minutes from the Rutgers campus, and the Scarlet Knight coaches liked keeping tabs on local players. One time, they were looking at film of a running back from a different high school but kept seeing a scrappy Colonia High middle linebacker making huge tackles on their hotshot prospect. A defensive coach asked Coach Schiano to take a look at the film, and based on the five open-field tackles Eric made, the Rutgers staff offered him a full-ride scholarship—unprecedented for a high school freshman.

Of course, the offer couldn't be put into writing until Eric's junior year, but Coach Schiano was the first major college coach to recruit Eric to play football. News of the scholarship offer was met with disbelief from Eric as well as from his mother, who was raising her son as a single mom. Up until then, she had no idea how she could afford to send her son to college.

While Eric knew who his father was, he didn't grow up with a dad in the home. Karen introduced her son to male role models by putting him in various sports leagues and activities. Going into high school, Eric had been a top-notch running back and linebacker in Pop Warner football as well as a fireball pitcher and a big hitter on the baseball diamond.

At the end of his freshman year, Eric attended the Rutgers summer football camp, where he first met Coach Schiano. The two started forming a lasting bond with one another. Since Eric and Mom lived so close to the Rutgers' campus, they attended Scarlet Knights' games in the fall and witnessed firsthand the resurgence in Rutgers' football fortunes. In 2005, Rutgers finished with a 7–4 record and qualified for its first bowl game in twenty-seven years.

Suddenly, Rutgers football was exciting again, and the bandwagon got crowded when the Scarlet Knights won their first eight games of the 2006 season. Eric was among the thousands of delirious students who rushed onto the field after Rutgers beat Top 10-ranked Louisville on a last-second field goal during an ESPN-televised Thursday night game. In the days that followed, Eric imagined that he would one day be part of an awesome postgame celebration like that. Coach Schiano, always recruiting, reminded Eric that there was a place for him at Rutgers.

Eric dominated high school play and became a highly prized recruit following his junior season, and schools like Notre Dame, Florida, Virginia, and Miami sought him out with full-ride offers. Fighting Irish coach Charlie Weis even showed up at Colonia High to make his pitch, which had the hallways buzzing.

With blue-chip recruits like Eric, college coaches often seek a verbal commitment in the late spring of the player's junior year of high school. On cue, Coach Schiano called in late May and reminded Eric that Rutgers University had been recruiting him since his freshman year and had been looking out for him the entire way. "We really want you to come to Rutgers," Schiano said. "We're on the verge of something big. We were 11–2 last season and ranked No. 12. We want you to be part of the excitement at Scarlet Nation, which is why I need to know where your head is. Have you made a decision? Can we count on you?"

Eric stuttered and asked for a timeout. He needed to speak with his mother first. Eric was a junior in high school and just sixteen years old at the time, so this was a big decision.

When Eric called back and told Coach Schiano that he was committing to Rutgers, the coach used the moment to teach Eric something about what it means to make a commitment, even if it was not in writing.

"So you're telling me that you're giving me your word?" the coach asked. "Only men give their word and really mean it and keep it."

Eric got the message to man up. "Coach, I'm giving you my word. I know that I might be a young man, but I'm giving you my word that I'm coming to Rutgers. And I'm not changing my mind."

The coach exhaled a sigh of relief. "Eric LeGrand, let me be the first to welcome you to Rutgers University. Congratulations. You are now part of the Rutgers football family."

A TERRIBLE REALITY

When Coach Schiano heard the *crack* of bone and vertebrae, he sensed this wasn't going to end well. "It didn't take me very long to run out there because I knew something wasn't right," he said.

The first thing he noticed was how rapidly Eric was going

into shock. "From the look in his eyes, he was really scared. His legs were raised off the ground, and he was stiff. As soon as I got to him, I said, 'Slow down. Slow everything down. You're going to be okay.' I tried to be calm and pray over him. I saw that he wasn't going to sit up."

Schiano had the presence of mind to know that his mother needed to be there, which is why he asked an assistant go find her. So why did he say "Just pray" to Eric's mother? Because he saw the fear in her eyes. "I couldn't say 'He's going to be okay' because I knew he wasn't going to be okay," Schiano said.

Every coach's worst nightmare—seeing one of his players paralyzed on the field of play—was now Greg Schiano's reality. What happened to Eric on October 16, 2010, weighed heavily on him and the Rutgers football program. After the Scarlet Knights rallied to beat Army in overtime, they lost their last six games of the 2010 season, unable to shake themselves from the black cloud that hung over the team. Coach Schiano told the media that what happened to Eric made the rest of the 2010 season a challenge, but that it also drew the players together. He said he believed there would be a lot of positives ahead for Eric, for his family, and for everyone associated with Rutgers football.

Schiano continued to visit his injured player at the Kessler Institute for Rehabilitation, where Eric regained some of his strength and learned how to move around in a $40,000 Permobil wheelchair, which he could steer by pressing a mouthpiece with his lips. Coach continued to phone Eric several times a week to check up on him.

A few weeks before the start of the 2011 Rutgers football season, Coach Schiano called Eric and told him that he'd like him to lead the team out of the tunnel and onto the field at one of the team's home games. Eric could pick the date.

That simple request bolstered Eric's spirits. He was dealing with the reality that he couldn't move his arms or his legs, and this was something to look *forward* to. Eric asked Greg if he could think about it.

When Coach called back a few days later, Eric said he would be honored to lead the team onto the field before the West Virginia game on October 29, 2011. The Mountaineers were a Top 20 team and had Rutgers' number, having beaten the Scarlet Knights *sixteen* consecutive times. Eric thought that if he led his old teammates onto the field of battle, it would inspire them to something special that day.

Then Schiano took it upon himself to lift Eric's spirits again. He made some behind-the-scenes arrangements for Eric to become part of the Rutgers radio broadcast team, offering his analysis in pregame, halftime, and postgame reports. Eric had always said his dream was to play in the NFL and then become a broadcaster when he retired from the game, and here was his chance to get some on-the-job training in the broadcast booth.

When it became time for Eric to lead his old team onto the field, though, things didn't turn out the way they drew it up on the blackboard, as they say in football.

Here's how most people wish it would have gone: As a sell-out crowd rose to its feet in appreciation of the fallen hero, Eric would slowly roll onto the field in front of eighty Scarlet Knights and the coaching staff. Then, playing their hearts out under a canopy of Indian summer sunshine, the Rutgers players would fight back from a fourth-quarter deficit to deliver a special victory. With a sixteen-game losing streak thrown into the dustbin, thousands of rowdy Rutgers fans would storm the field and hoist the heroic football team on their shoulders. And, of course, the Rutgers players would all agree that Eric had inspired them to new heights.

But here's what really happened: a freak pre-Halloween storm hit Rutgers Stadium on the morning of the late-afternoon game, depositing two inches of snow on the field. A lot of fans stayed in their warm homes, so the stands were barely half full. Those who did come to the game wore thick coats and hopped from one foot to another as snow flurries swirled through the darkening sky.

Eric was pushed through the slosh to the entrance of the Rutgers locker room, and he was freezing. When his team finally came out of the locker room, following a momentary delay, cheers rose in the throats of 20,000 fans as two of Eric's old teammates placed a red-handled axe across his wheelchair's armrests. They wanted to show Rutgers fans that Eric was "still chopping," a rallying cry used by Schiano to keep the effort high on every hike of the ball. *Don't let up. Keep chopping.*

A slow procession took the team to midfield, where they made a right turn toward the Rutgers bench. Once the loose scrum reached the sidelines, Coach Schiano gathered everyone around Eric and asked everyone to bow their heads. "God, please heal this man!" he cried out. "Please let him walk again!"

"Amen!" replied his teammates in unison.

Coach Schiano then broke the team's huddle with a chant that had become familiar to every Rutgers football player: "It's family on three . . . one, two, three—FAMILY!"

The fired-up Scarlet Knights took a 31–21 lead into half-time, but a fourth-quarter West Virginia rally sealed a 35–31 Rutgers loss. A bitter seventeenth-consecutive defeat at the hands of the Mountaineers was in the books.

Even though it wasn't the storybook ending so many had hoped for, God used that miserable afternoon in Piscataway for His glory. A few weeks after the game, *Sports Illustrated* announced that it would be doing something never done before in the magazine's fifty-seven-year history: allow fans to choose the Best Sports Moment of 2011 for the cover of its year-end double issue.

The image of Eric, wearing a red wool cap and team sweats as he led his team onto a snowy field was picked as one of the fifteen nominations. Fans could vote online, and in the end, Eric's emotional rollout against West Virginia beat out Aaron Rodgers leading the Green Bay Packers to a Super Bowl victory and Derek Jeter becoming the first New York Yankee to amass 3,000 hits.

That was a big deal. I believe that because Eric LeGrand graced the cover of *Sports Illustrated* in late 2011, the big New York publisher, William Morrow/HarperCollins, moved forward with the *Believe* book project. Eric was able to share in his book that even though he can't shake a hand, walk across a street, or use a remote control, he can still point people to God because he really believes that the Lord has a plan for his life, even with this horrible injury.

A DEPARTURE AND A DRAFT

At the same time the compelling photo of Eric's entrance onto the snowy Rutgers football field graced newsstands across America, the Tampa Bay Buccaneers were looking for a new head coach. The team had suffered through a horrible 4–12 season in 2011, and the organization was looking for a defensive-minded, no-nonsense coach to change the culture in Tampa Bay.

This wasn't the first time Schiano had been wooed for an NFL job, but this time he listened. His four kids were getting older—they ranged in age from fifteen to nine—so it seemed as good a time as any to make a major move.

But if you know Greg Schiano, you know he doesn't believe in making any big decision unilaterally. This was a matter that impacted his entire family, so he called for a family meeting to let the four kids know that he and Mom were on the verge of accepting the Tampa Bay job.

One of their twin boys raised his hand. "What about Eric?" he asked.

Greg and Christy looked at each other. They hadn't expected this reaction. "Well, Eric will come and visit and stay with us when he comes to our games," the coach replied.

When Eric heard the news that Coach Schiano was leaving Rutgers, he understood that it was a good decision for his old coach and his family. When Schiano called Eric, he reminded his former player that moving to another part of the country to take a new coaching job didn't change anything between them and that he was still in this for life with Eric.

Tasked with rebuilding the Tampa Bay team, Coach Schiano assembled a staff and went to work preparing for the 2012 NFL draft. What happened following the draft showed Coach Schiano's heart to a nation of football fans.

Remember Mike McCartney—the Chicago Bears director

of college scouting who led Schiano to Christ when he handed him that cassette tape of his father's preaching? McCartney had since become a player's agent, and as the NFL draft
approached, he called the new Tampa Bay coach with an
idea: Why not, after the seventh and final round of the draft,
allow one more player to be drafted—a player not expected
to ever play in the NFL but one who had been living through
difficult life circumstances? Why not make that special pick
Eric LeGrand, who, had he not suffered that tragic injury,
just might have been part of the 2012 draft class?

Coach Schiano loved the idea, and so did Bucs' general
manager Mark Dominik. But as often happens in life, Mc
Cartney's proposal got lost in the tyranny of the urgent and
was never passed along to NFL headquarters in New York
City. The draft came and went, but the idea of doing *something* for Eric never left Schiano's mind.

Then Coach Schiano had another brainstorm—the
team could sign Eric as a free agent and invite him to training camp. He could receive a No. 52 Bucs jersey, be part of
a team, and technically "retire" as an NFL player. Now that
was something the Buccaneers *could* do, and they didn't even
need the NFL's permission.

Here's how Eric and I described it in his book:

> I had no inkling what was up when Coach called
> in a chatty mood the following day. We were talk
> ing football when he changed the subject. "I want
> to sign you as one of our free agents," he blurted.
>
> I didn't think I heard right. "Are you seri
> ous?" I asked. "You're going to waste a spot on

me?" I knew that all NFL teams were limited to a ninety-man roster going into training camp.

"This is something I want to do," Coach replied. "I talked to the GM and our owner, and everyone is on board."

I wasn't aware of this conversation until later, which is why I thought my eyes were playing tricks on me when I saw the online headline: Eric LeGrand Fulfills NFL Dreams by Signing with Tampa Bay Buccaneers and Greg Schiano. This was in early May 2012, when I was in the midst of writing *Believe*. I was blown away by the humanity of Schiano's gesture, and I knew what the recognition would mean to the young man in the wheelchair.

I also had a great ending to the book, which was a godsend. Wanting to flesh out the coach's thought process a bit, I asked Eric if he could arrange for me to interview Greg Schiano. I wanted his perspective on why he chose to honor Eric with a symbolic free agent contract.

When we connected by phone, Schiano reminisced about Eric. Coach told me several stories, including one of Eric as a freshman on the kickoff return team. He had knocked down one of the coverage men, and to keep him from getting back up, Eric stood spread-legged over his opponent.

After a good laugh in the film room on Sunday, Coach Schiano said, "Eric, you can't do that. You can't stop him from getting up."

"Okay, Coach," a chastened Eric replied.

The stories were fun, but then I walked Coach Schiano through the events of October 10, 2010. I was impressed with the way he shared memories of those painfully difficult days.

"I'm sorry I'm making you relive this," I said.

"Me reliving it? This kid lives it every day," Schiano replied. He made it clear that no one should feel sorry for him as the coach.

In time, our conversation veered to a notion that Schiano had been considering—to do away with the traditional kick-off, replacing it with a play that would greatly decrease the chances of another young man like Eric LeGrand being paralyzed during a play.

During those long evenings at Hackensack's medical center, Schiano had lots of time to think. *Is there something that can be done to make the kickoff safer?* He knew the kick-off and the onside kick were among the most dangerous plays in football. Schiano's research revealed that kickoffs—accounted for 6 percent of all plays—led to *17 percent* of the game's catastrophic injuries.

It stands to reason—the kickoff is a bad accident just waiting to happen. You begin with players lining up five to seven yards behind the kickoff line so they can sprint past the tee the instant the kicker swings his leg. As the ball sails through the air, the coverage team players are running downfield as fast as they can, dodging blockers, working together to bring down the return man.

In the mayhem of the moment, there are high-speed collisions that can cause horrific injuries. Fans utter an *Ooooh!* when a player gets laid out. But think about the guy who just had his brains scrambled—or his knee shredded—from a vicious hit.

If there was ever a moment for thinking outside the box,

Schiano thought this was it. He challenged himself to devise an exciting way to start play at the beginning of each half and after every score.

What if . . .

A question crossed the coach's mind: What happens when there's a safety? Answer: Play resumes with a punt from the 20-yard line.

What if . . .

What if, when a team scores a touchdown or a field goal, it immediately got the ball back on its own 30-yard line? But it wouldn't be a first-and-ten situation—this would be fourth down, with 15 yards to go.

This was Greg Schiano's idea.

Think of the possibilities. Most teams, of course, would send out their punting units. But it's not a free kick. The receiving team could block the punt . . . or the punting team might try a fake.

But let's say your team is down four points with less than two minutes to play. You're out of time-outs. Since there's no longer an onside kick option, the coach will send his offense onto the field for a fourth-and-fifteen play—which can be a run, a pass, a bootleg, or something razzle-dazzle. The permutations are endless, just like any other desperation fourth-and-fifteen play. Make at least fifteen yards, and you get a fresh set of downs and chance to drive for the winning score. Fall short, and the other team gets the ball at the point of the spot.

I *love* Schiano's fourth-and-fifteen idea. Sure, eliminating the kickoff would be a major rule change, but football can handle it. Younger readers won't remember this, but in 1996 college football did something revolutionary by introducing an overtime rule that gave each team a chance to score from the 25-yard line. Fans had to get used to this unconventional method of breaking ties—and determining a winner in every game.

Now, the college overtime is one of the most exciting ways to determine a winner in any sport—better even than the "sudden death" NFL version, in my opinion. Pro football's overtime rules were tweaked in 2012 to give the trailing team at least one possession unless the first team with the ball scores a touchdown or a safety. But the NFL overtime is played just like the first sixty minutes of football, and regular season games can still end in a tie.

Schiano told me that he had buttonholed NFL Commissioner Roger Goodell, "and I know this idea is getting traction. I know the commissioner is concerned about protecting the players in these dangerous play situations."

That's why we saw Goodell send up a trial balloon at the end of the 2012 season when he gave an interview to *Time* magazine. In that conversation, Goodell said he and the NFL's competition committee were considering whether to replace the kickoff with Schiano's fourth-and-fifteen idea.

Schiano's suggestion hasn't been warmly welcomed by fans, and kickoff rule changes may be years away. But I wouldn't be surprised if we saw it tried out in preseason games in 2014 or 2015. Schiano's idea would introduce another layer of strategy to the great game of football, which is constantly changing and evolving.

I'd like to suggest that this rule change have a name. I'm sure Coach Schiano would agree with me on this:

The LeGrand Rule.

8

TERRELL FLETCHER:
THE HEART OF A CHAPLAIN

As I prepared a list of those I wanted to interview and feature in this edition of *Playing with Purpose*, I decided to focus some attention on one of the thirty-two chaplains in the NFL.

You don't hear much about NFL chaplains, but every team has one. They are unpaid volunteers who make themselves available to talk with players any time, day or night, and who are responsible for holding chapel services in the players' hotel (home and away) on the eve of games.

The days of pro football players driving themselves to home games on a Sunday morning ended with the Nixon administration. Today's NFL coaches don't like leaving anything to chance, and that includes having their players out footloose and fancy free on a Saturday night. Thus, the players are required to drive their cars to the stadium on Saturday afternoon, where a bus waits to take them to a nearby Hyatt- or Marriott-type hotel.

Players spend the night in the team hotel and participate in a series of meetings and meals on Saturday night and Sunday morning. Typically, there is an 11 p.m. curfew, when coaches come knocking on doors to make sure players haven't snuck out—or furtively smuggled a woman into their rooms.

"Bed check," it's called.

Another Saturday night tradition is team chapel, which usually takes place in one of the hotel conference rooms. Chapel services, which can take the shape of a short sermon or a Bible study with prayer time, generally last around forty-five minutes. Attendance is voluntary, and from what I've been told, between fifteen and thirty players, coaches, and team personnel—sometimes a few more—show up for the services around the league.

I live in San Diego, so I naturally sought out the Chargers' team chaplain, Terrell Fletcher. Terrell played eight seasons in the Chargers' backfield in the '90s and early '00s. He was a small guy by NFL standards, a 5-foot, 8-inch, 196-pound scatback whose lightning-quick moves on the field often left defenders grasping at air.

Terrell gave his life to Christ when he was a senior at the University of Wisconsin and was outspoken about his faith during his professional football career. His teammates knew not to even bother asking him to go clubbing or picking up women.

After retiring from football in 2003, Terrell attended San Diego Bible College to work on his theological degree and also worked as a youth pastor. He married his wife, Sheree, following graduation from Bible college and founded the City of Hope International Church, where he is the senior pastor leading a thriving multicultural congregation. Terrell's motivating messages have made him a sought-after speaker around the country and in nations like Nigeria, Cote d'Ivoire, Uganda, and Belize. In the summer of 2012, he became the Chargers chaplain, succeeding Shawn Mitchell, who'd been on call for twenty-eight years. Terrell had some big loafers to fill.

I caught up with Terrell late in the 2012 season, and we had the following conversation:

When some people hear the title "team chaplain," they think it's some type of ceremonial position. Do you sense that when you introduce yourself?

Terrell: I think there's a perception that NFL chaplains are not that involved with the players, that we just show up and do a chapel service or Bible study before the game and then we disappear.

It's really not like that. In many ways, we're chosen to be their pastors, at least during the season. We carry a great burden for the guys. We pray for them and with them. We pray for their families. We challenge them.

Even the players who don't come to the chapel services, we're still connected to their lives. They'll ask for a private moment after practice, or they'll grab you as you're walking out onto the football field before a game. For the most part, though, I don't think people know exactly what chaplains do and what our responsibilities are.

Team chaplains are listed in the teams' media guides with a bio and picture, so there's something official about the position. What support does the team give you as a chaplain?

Terrell: The Chargers have been extremely gracious to me. They've given me great access to the guys. They've supplied me with the freedom to connect with the coaches. They've given me personal information and phone numbers so I can connect with everyone outside of football if they so desire. I've been very fortunate because I've heard nightmare stories about chaplains on other teams who weren't given as much access to the players. One chaplain was not allowed to travel with the team to away games.

The Chargers organization wants the chaplain to be a resource to the players and coaches. I'm invited to drop by the practice facility, which I do once or twice a week so that the guys can come grab me, ask for prayer . . . whatever.

You mentioned that some other chaplains have challenges or maybe even roadblocks. What does that look like?

Terrell: As a Christian chaplain, if you can't preach the Christian message in its entirety, then you might as well not even show up. The Chargers have no restrictions on the message I share with the guys, unlike some other situations I've heard about around the league.

When I took the chaplaincy over from a wonderful man of God, Shawn Mitchell, one of the things he challenged me with was this: "Make sure you give them the gospel of Jesus Christ. Challenge their lives because we don't want them to just be good football players. We're called to help them become godly men."

Sometimes the challenge in professional sports is to leave faith and religion out of the sport and to only use faith and religion as a good-luck charm that helps them make that catch in traffic or score in the red zone. That's not what I do. The Chargers organization understands that we have Christians on the team who are seeking godly counsel, so they give me access to the players. I have the ability to walk through the locker room, check in with the guys, shake hands, say "What's up?" and then escort them to a private room nearby if they want to talk about a private matter.

If you're a chaplain, you need to have some kind of access and flexibility to share the full gospel, and the Chargers have provided that.

HOW ARE TEAM CHAPLAINS SUPPORTED?

Since NFL teams do not pay chaplains, how can they afford to volunteer their time with the players?

NFL chaplains generally fit into three categories:

• they are on staff with a sports ministry like Athletes in Action or Fellowship of Christian Athletes and raise their own support

• they are full-time pastors who have the support of their church behind them

• they are former players who saved their money well and can support themselves

Do you travel to every away game?

Terrell: The Chargers allow me to fly on the team plane so that I can be there for road games and conduct chapel on the night before the game. During the 2012 season, I only traveled to four away games because I still pastor a church and can't be gone eight weeks out of the seventeen-week season.

When I don't travel to an away game, I make provisions for speakers to cover for me. Let's say the Chargers are playing in Indianapolis. Then I'm going to call Tony Dungy and see if he'll come and do a chapel service for us.

Here in San Diego, I've brought in Miles McPherson on Saturday nights. Miles played several years for the Chargers and pastors the Rock Church, which has a congregation of 12,000. He's also quite an evangelist who speaks all around the country. Sometimes guys need to hear a different voice and a different perspective.

Let's walk through a typical week during the season, starting with Monday. What kinds of things happen on the day after each game?

Terrell: The guys have a short practice on Monday, so every other Monday, we do a home Bible fellowship. The guys will meet at one of the player's homes, and we'll do a Bible study and have pizza and salad. There's a lot of feedback and conversation among the players, who express things on their hearts. We also pray for one another, and the prayer requests give me a pulse on the team.

There are no wives and girlfriends on Monday nights. Just athletes. We try to focus on the guys. We have a young group, and sometimes—and this is a hazard of the job—the girlfriends come and go. The girlfriend in Week 1 might be very different than the girlfriend in Week 9. Sometimes a coach will join us, and I'll bring in somebody from our church to share his testimony.

Tuesday is an off day for everybody, and everyone needs

a day off once a week to chill out and let the body heal.

On Wednesdays, I'll show up at the Chargers' training facility during the middle of practice, where I'll watch the guys. When the final whistle blows, we'll have a group prayer on the field. Guys will come together, just like they do after the game on Sundays, to pray in the middle of the field. About fifteen, twenty, maybe twenty-five guys will go to one knee in the prayer circle, and I'll pray that God will bless the team, heal us from our injuries, and keep our minds focused on Him. It's a public display of our faith to their teammates as well as to the coaches, but we've had coaches join us in that prayer circle and even management, too.

After practice, I hang out in the locker room and catch up with the guys. There's a room nearby that's available if a guy needs some extra time with me. We had an incident this season where a player was going through a very tough situation. The coaching staff was gracious enough to let him skip a meeting to have that time with me. That's a rarity in the NFL.

Thursdays and Fridays, we are always available for the guys to call or text, and they will do that. I sometimes hear from them. Saturday is when we do the team chapel, usually starting at 6 p.m. We're allotted forty-five minutes to do a quick lesson.

Sundays are game day. I'm at the stadium, hanging around the locker room before kickoff, but I give the guys their space. Some will seek me out, though. They call me "Rev," as in . . . *Rev, I want you to pray real quick.* Then I'm asked to lead the entire team in a short prayer just before we leave the locker room for the player introductions. During the game, I stand on the sidelines near the team bench and try to stay out of the way, but I'm always available for a quick word of encouragement.

When the game is over, players and coaches from both teams gather in a prayer circle at the 50-yard line, which is voluntary and a public witness. At home, I lead that prayer. At away games, the host chaplain does it. When I reach the locker room with the players, the head coach always has a few postgame words and then he asks me to close in prayer. I'm there to deliver that.

Then it starts all over on Monday with a home Bible study, but like any pastor, I'm always available to have a conversation. They've got my cell number.

What do the players usually want to talk to you about?

Terrell: Relationship issues and dealing with the pressures of the job. The relationship issues are ongoing. Football players deal with stuff just like other human beings. The problems that athletes face are the same as everyone else. They're still figuring out this relationship thing. Security is their livelihood. We talk about football, the business of football, or the chances of injuries and how that relates to their livelihood and their income. It can go as far as personal issues, like tragedies in their lives, losing loved ones, or children who are ill.

Fans put professional football players on a pedestal, like they are modern-day gladiators. Well, they need a savior, too. God has given me an opportunity to express the love of Christ and remind them that *Hey, God is with you, too.*

How do you handle the issue of drinking and night-clubbing?

Terrell: I challenge godly men to be godly men. The choices and decisions that the players make are ones they have to own. I remind them that the testimony of a Christian's life should be one that honors God and exemplifies His grace over his life.

It's a value thing. How do you value how you represent Christ? How do you value what spiritual transformation and growth is like in your life? Is going out nightclubbing and drinking excessively befitting of the commitment you want to make?

I also show them Scriptures where alcohol is damaging, such as Proverbs 23:31–35 (New Living Translation):

> Don't gaze at the wine, seeing how red it is, how it sparkles in the cup, how smoothly it goes down.
>
> For in the end it bites like a poisonous snake; it stings like a viper.
>
> You will see hallucinations, and you will say crazy things.
>
> You will stagger like a sailor tossed at sea, clinging to a swaying mast.
>
> And you will say, "They hit me, but I didn't feel it. I didn't even know it when they beat me up. When will I wake up so I can look for another drink?"

I'll show them Scriptures where putting your good in an evil position hurts your testimony of what Christ is trying to do in your life. I'll explain how the transforming power of the Holy Spirit should transform their hearts toward the image of God.

I stay away from the "Don't do it" because I do know how athletes are wired and how men are wired, but I challenge them with this: "Hey, man, every decision you make, whether it's nightclubbing, who you're dating, how you are enjoying yourself—it's very important that you keep these ideas at the forefront of your heart and your mind, that you represent Christ and that your heart is transforming to the image of Christ."

The players are listening. The Chargers during the 2012 season had the least amount of off-the-field incidents as any Chargers team in recent history. That's how amazing this team was off the field. Not the product we wanted on the field, but the character of the guys was just a different deal. Nothing major happened.

Don't get me wrong. We've had stuff happen. I've had to grab guys, pray and talk with them. I push those guys in the areas of morality. "We're all not perfect, but you're a godly man," I say. I explain that it's an art letting the Holy Spirit challenge your heart and for you to acquiesce and say yes to the Holy Spirit, who nudges their hearts not to go there.

"God cares about every aspect of your life," I'll say. "You don't want to minimize God down to the Big Three: don't drink, don't smoke, and don't sleep around. God wants to be involved in your whole life. In every aspect of your life, He has an opinion on that. Listen to Him when you read Scripture, and listen to His voice when He challenges your heart. Respond to it, man. You have done well if you sense you shouldn't be in a certain place tonight and gone back to your place or your hotel alone. That's honoring God."

Another hot-button issue with the guys has to be the easy availability of premarital sex. I would imagine that you're talking to them about that topic until you're blue in the face. Am I right on that?

Terrell: Sex is easily available to the guys. It doesn't help matters that the world has put sex out for sale. We do everything by the allure of sex.

Helping guys guard their "eye gates" so that they don't make bad choices is one of the top conversations I have, but it isn't easy because men in general don't open up and talk a lot. And they *really* don't open up and talk about their failures.

So if a person fails in the area of premarital sex and makes a mistake, I try to keep the ground open so that there is conversation between us. I don't want him to feel like there is condemnation coming from me. Instead, I talk about the importance of having accountability with someone he trusts and setting some parameters and backstops up so he doesn't find himself in the same situation a few weeks later.

The premarital sex thing is a real grind for the players, a real struggle. I know because I lived that. When I played, I had great accountability around me. I made up my mind and heart that I was going to try to do it God's way, and I was fortunate to get out unscathed.

Keep in mind that there are a bunch of issues at work here. Sometimes sex is not just about lust. There's also the issue of single-parented men who still identify their manliness with the easiest thing for them to conquer, and many times it's a woman. Many times it's not about having sex but that *I got her*. It's a win.

There are a lot of guys in the NFL who didn't have male figures in their lives when they grew up. When a boy is sixteen or seventeen, and he wants to start to express his male qualities, he's looking for something to win. When you're a good athlete, a nice-looking kid, have a unique gift or talent that makes you attractive to the girls, it's an easy victory. For some guys, it's not about the sex part. It's *I conquered the mountain. I won.*

The whole sex thing is really layered. How do you help a guy feel solid outside of being a football player? When he's twenty-five years old, he's probably been told that he's a great football player since he was fourteen. There aren't many other ways to prove himself in the world, so we create these societies of guys where bravado and victory is built around being the best football player, the best athlete, and the most attractive to girls, instead of creating a world that is centered around God and His purpose for your life.

When you have purpose in your life, you're seeking God. When you don't have purpose, then you're looking for women to satisfy you, or things that money can buy, or going out and nightclubbing. That's a never-ending cycle because those things were never meant to feed you, never meant to fill that void in your heart. The only thing that truly satisfies is walking with God.

You've mentioned accountability in your playing days. What does that look like?

Terrell: Some of the guys have set up good accountability measures. They'll room together. They'll do bed checks together. They'll knock on a hotel door and say, "Hey, man, are we in the room by ourselves?" That kind of deal.

Guys need to look after each other. I know that was a big help to me. When I was at the University of Wisconsin, one of the team chaplains knew I had given my life to the Lord.

When I got drafted and came out to San Diego, he called Shawn Mitchell, the Chargers chaplain, and said we have a new Christian coming, so keep an eye out for him.

Shawn grabbed four or five guys and said, "Hey, when Terrell Fletcher gets into the locker room, will you just love on him?"

I didn't know any of this was going to happen, but when I arrived at my first minicamp, four or five guys, including kicker John Carney and running back Rodney Culver, met me in the locker room with this message: *Hey, we love God. We heard that you recently gave your life to the Lord and made a commitment to Him. We want to help you with your commitment because it can be done in the NFL.*

They wrote down their phone numbers. They said to call them at any time. That was the kind of fellowship that I walked into in the NFL.

Now I wasn't a great Christian initially, but when I learned the value of what the Scriptures teach in Ecclesiastes 4:9–12, that two are better than one, and when a brother falls, the other is there to pick him up, I can't tell you how invaluable that was to me.

That's something I try to bring to the guys and the idea that accountability is a choice you make. I tell them they can do things that no one will ever learn about. What a great testimony it is to be able to say that you love God and want to walk with Him with pure hands and a clean heart.

Some of those guys have taken advantage of that with each other, but it's a journey. I get to walk the journey with these guys.

CHAPLAIN WIVES PLAY A ROLE, TOO

With many NFL teams, the team chaplain is a two-for-one proposition: the chaplain's wife often ministers to the wives of players and coaches, holding Bible studies for them and being a reliable source of support.

A chaplain's wife participates in couples' Bible studies with the players and their wives and is often a bulwark when a player's wife calls with news of an injury, a trade, or an outright release. She holds hands and cries with young women who've suffered a miscarriage or the loss of a parent.

Just as it's not easy being an NFL wife, it's not easy being the wife of a chaplain.

I would imagine the Parable of the Sower resonates with you. You plant seeds with the players. Some seed falls on rocky ground, some falls among thorns, and some falls on good soil. Is that a good parable for what you do?

Terrell: That is the perfect parable. I am a sower of seeds in the NFL. All my chaplain brothers are sowers.

Sure, some of the seeds we throw fall by the wayside—among players who show no interest in learning how Jesus died for their sins so that they can have eternal life. Other seeds fail to penetrate the stony hearts of players, which prevents the Word of God from making an impression. Some of my seeds fall amid the thorns, meaning that these seeds take root for a while, but the riches and pleasures of life in the NFL choke their growth. I see that happen time and time again, which grieves me, but I prefer to remember the seeds that have fallen on good soil, resulting in tons of spiritual growth and changed lives.

You see, my role as a chaplain is to share God's love and grace with whoever will listen—"whoever has ears to hear, let him hear"—and pray that the seeds of God's message of salvation would pierce their hearts. Scripture tells us that no one comes to the Father unless the Spirit draws them. If there is a spiritual awakening that takes place, then it's God work, not our work.

My job is not so much to get them to hear the message as much as making the information available. Sometimes, though, it does feel like the seeds fall on hard ground, and that's disheartening.

As a believer, I know that Jesus is the answer. I know that He will never leave you or forsake you. To see that rejected can be disappointing and even hurtful. It even makes me mad, but then I remember that they are not rejecting me but the One who sent me. That hurts because we have such a powerful answer, but that hurt is tempered by great joy when one says yes to Christ or rededicates his life to the Lord.

Don't get me wrong. There's a lot of joy in being an NFL chaplain. We keep praying for each other, and there are lots and lots of victories we have seen. We give the rest to God. I believe that we plant seeds with every player we see, and perhaps some other time someone else will come along to love on them and take them to their next place in their journey.

SATURDAY NIGHT LIVE

I had one more question for Terrell: Could I sit in on a team chapel to see what goes on?

Terrell said he needed to check with the Chargers first.

He called back the next day, a Friday, and told me to meet him at the team hotel, not far from the stadium.

Little did we both know what would transpire in less than twenty-four hours. The following morning, a Saturday, I woke up to shocking news that rocked the NFL and sent ripples throughout the country: Jovan Belcher, a Kansas City Chiefs linebacker, had fired nine bullets into his girlfriend, the mother of his three-month-old daughter, killing her. He then drove over to Arrowhead Stadium, where he parked next to the practice facility. The first person he saw was Chiefs general manager Scott Pioli. Belcher stepped out of his Bentley and pointed his gun toward his head. "I did it," he said, according to the police report. "I killed her."

Pioli knew Belcher was having problems with his girlfriend. He tried to persuade Belcher to lay down his weapon, but the Chiefs player wouldn't drop the gun. Belcher asked if Pioli and owner Clark Hunt would take care of his daughter.

Chiefs head coach Romeo Crennel and linebackers coach Gary Gibbs arrived in the parking lot in plenty of time for the first team meeting of the day. Alarmed by the sight of one of their players holding a gun to his head, they sought to intervene.

Crennel told his player that everything could be worked out and that he still had a chance.

Police sirens sounded in the distance. The law was closing in.

"I got to go," Belcher said, according to the police report. "I can't be here."

The 6-foot, 2-inch, 228-pound linebacker knelt behind a vehicle, made the sign of the cross across his chest, pointed the handgun at his head, and pulled the trigger, firing a single bullet.

(An autopsy would reveal that his blood alcohol content was 0.17, more than twice the limit of 0.08 percent for Missouri drivers, so he had been drinking heavily the night before.)

THE SAN DIEGO CURSE?

When Terrell Fletcher made the Chargers roster in 1995, the team was coming off its first—and only—Super Bowl appearance, a dispiriting 49–26 loss to the San Francisco 49ers.

Little did Terrell know that eight of his teammates would die before the age of forty-five from causes ranging from a plane crash to a lightning strike to heart attacks.

And one by his own hand.

The first to depart was Terrell's roommate and Christian brother, Rodney Culver, who died eighteen months after the Super Bowl when he was aboard a ValuJet DC-9 that plunged into the Florida Everglades. Linebacker Doug Miller was also in the wrong place at the wrong time; he was struck by two bolts of lightning in the Colorado Rockies. Two teammates, Shawn Lee and Lew Bush, died of heart attacks.

The death—suicide, actually—of Junior Seau in May 2012 is the latest addition to a grim roll call. "I saw Junior a week before he died at his charity golf tournament," Terrell said. "That one was difficult to swallow. There was no indication. If anybody said he saw it coming . . . ."

When I arrived at the Chargers team hotel in the early evening, news of the murder/suicide was reverberating through the 24-hour news cycle. There were no "Welcome, Chargers!" signs inside the hotel lobby. In fact, there were barely any people around. I waited a couple of minutes, and then Terrell found me. He had been sitting in the hotel restaurant.

He led me to a stairway leading downstairs, where I spotted

someone with the Chargers, not dressed in team colors, checking out people as they passed by. Nearby, a sign leading to several ballrooms and conference rooms read, "Private Party." Everything was low key.

Terrell led me inside a small conference room, where I took a seat in the last row—only to see Chargers safety Corey Lynch sitting in front of me. I counted twelve players, a handful of coaches, and a team trainer inside the small partitioned room. We were just steps away from the main ballroom where the entire team had participated in a meeting that afternoon—and would gather one more time that evening, after the forty-minute chapel service was over.

After opening in prayer, Terrell said that when he woke up this morning, he had a different message in mind: "My heart was set on teaching about what it means to get back up as a team, focus and all that during the dog days of the season, and then I got a text message saying, 'What do you know about this Kansas City situation?'

"I knew this would be a major ripple through the NFL, that every team would have to deal with it. This happened during the season, it happened at the team stadium, this happened with a player who was a starter, and I'd be remiss if I didn't ask God what I'm supposed to share with my brothers at this chapel event.

"I'm driving in, and I'm thinking, *Don't let your heart be troubled.* I don't know what happened in Jovan Belcher's life, and there isn't much information available, but it seems like what happened is he and his girlfriend got into an argument. He got so enraged that he shot and killed her.

"He realized he made a mistake. He went to the safest place

he knew, which was the football stadium. And that's where he took his own life. He apparently didn't see a way out.

"Now, why do I say this?" Terrell asked. "Because there was a time when I didn't see a way out."

It happened before Terrell's sophomore season at the University of Wisconsin. He walked into a nightclub and started drinking—something he had been doing since he was fourteen years old. Then Terrell and his friends got into an argument with some other patrons in the bar. Words were exchanged, things escalated, and then fists started flying. "We got into a fight, and I all I wanted to do was bloody his nose and bust his lip so that the guys would say that I was the man," he recounted.

The fight got ugly, and the cops were called. Next thing Terrell knew, he was fighting a two-year jail sentence, a $10,000 fine, and the loss of his scholarship—and his promising football career. "My parents had less than $18,000 left to pay on their house, but they had to borrow every cent they could to keep my dumb butt out of jail," he said to the Chargers players. "My heart was troubled."

Terrell got a second chance. He received probation, was ordered to do five hundred hours of community service, and was allowed to keep his football scholarship. A year later, he was walking across the quad at the University of Wisconsin when an older woman stopped him to share a Bible verse and a thought for the day: "Son, the devil is trying to sift you as wheat, but I'm going to pray for you."

The encounter shook Terrell and was the catalyst to him getting saved not long after that. His life changed in unimaginable ways, and for the better.

"So don't let your heart be troubled," Terrell told the players. "There's a Savior who can help you and put people around you who can help you. You don't have to end up like this young man in Kansas City."

Terrell turned thoughtful for a moment. "What would I have said to that young Chiefs player if I saw him in that parking lot with a gun? I would said, 'Hey, man, you made a mistake. But God can still do something incredible with your life. Let us help you. I don't care how you got where you are right now. Let somebody help you. Don't lose everything that's important because you didn't call for help.'"

Terrell then shared a special 800-number that NFL players and coaches could call to speak with a counselor about what had happened in Kansas City that day.

Time to wrap up. Terrell finished with a prayer. With heads bowed, the Chargers chaplain finished the chapel service on this note:

"Father, I thank You and bless You for my brothers. Father, when we hear stories like the guy in Kansas City, it seems like our small injuries seem relatively insignificant. Father, I'm not naïve, and You already know what we wrestle with and what we go through every day. Father, I pray that You will continue to transform our hearts in Your image, that You allow us to submit ourselves to accountability to one another and those who can help, and Father, I pray that we erase our pride, and that we ask for help when we need it, and that the right help will find its way to our lives. In Christ's name, we pray. Amen."

Terrell had one final message:

"Love you guys. Get a win tomorrow."

9

TWO-MINUTE WARNING:
JOHN CROYLE OF
THE BIG OAK RANCH

Unless you live in the state of Alabama, it's likely you've never heard of John Croyle, a stork-like defensive end for the Crimson Tide who used his considerable quickness and strength to terrorize opposing offensive backfields in the early 1970s.

John played for legendary coach Paul "Bear" Bryant, and everyone believed he had a bright future in professional football waiting for him. At 6 feet, 7 inches and a lean and mean 220 pounds, John had that special knack for getting off the ball quickly, slipping blocks, and sacking quarterbacks.

But when John's college career was over and the 1973 NFL draft approached, he was plagued with doubt—not doubt that he was good enough to play professional football but misgivings about whether it was the direction God had set for his life. Nobody knew John's secret ambition: to start a

Christian children's home for the orphaned, abused, neglected, and abandoned.

Torn between two dreams—pursuing an NFL career or starting a home for unwanted boys—he sought out ol' Bear Bryant for advice. Remembered for his tan, leathery face and a gravelly voice, Coach Bryant was a wise man who taught his players three things: sacrifice, work, and self-discipline. "I teach these things, and my boys don't forget them when they leave," he said.

When John explained the two roads that lay in front of him, the old coach put a hand on his shoulder. "You have to marry pro football to play it well, son," he said.

Bryant's words sealed John's decision because he knew what they meant—NFL coaches had a certain way of demanding every waking hour of their players' lives: meetings, practice, meal times, weight room, and more meetings. There was no "halfway" for an NFL player.

John removed his name from the draft and plowed ahead with his dream. A Birmingham doctor stepped up and gave him $15,000 in seed money, but John needed $30,000 more for a down payment on a ranch outside Gadsden. That happened to be the exact amount that a 'Bama teammate, John Hannah, received from the New England Patriots as his signing bonus in 1974. When John Hannah signed over his bonus check, the Big Oak Ranch was born.

I was editor of *Focus on the Family* magazine in the 1990s when acquaintances from Birmingham told me I really needed to check out the Big Oak Ranch and write a story about what was happening in Gadsden.

Twenty years had passed since John first received his state

license, purchased a small home on a lot of acreage, and taken in four boys from tough family backgrounds. Over those two decades, more homes had been built on the large property, and a girl's version of the Big Oak Ranch was launched forty-five minutes away. During those twenty years in the trenches, John had worked with 1,200 children. He told me that he had learned two things that all parents should know about their kids:

1. You love your children, no matter what
2. You believe in them, no matter what

But there were two things, he said, that children have a hard time forgiving their parents for, and they were:

1. Not disciplining them
2. Not trying

When I spoke with John on the phone, his self-deprecating humor and down-home storytelling rose to the surface. He told me harrowing stories of hearing cars coming onto the ranch property late at night, followed by doors slamming and tires squealing as a hopeless parent dropped off and abandoned another crying kid. There was the young boy whose mother had dipped him into a vat of boiling grease, and others with cigarette burns or ugly scars from knife wounds. John said that many of the children who found their way to Big Oak Ranch had never seen a toothbrush or slept in their own bed. They were malnourished physically and starved for love and attention as well.

"That's why when children come to the Big Oak Ranch, I tell them four things: one, I love you; two, I'll never lie to you; three, I'll stick with you till you're grown; and four, there are boundaries, so don't cross them.

"That may sound harsh, but what I give these children are four things: one, emotional support; two, honesty; three, endurance; and four, the knowledge that there are boundaries. Those are four things youngsters desperately want, and that includes your children as well."

I listened closely, and loved what I was hearing.

My children were in middle school at the time, and I thought allowing them to see something different than their cul-de-sac existence would be a great eye-opening experience. When we arrived in Alabama, we visited both Big Oak Ranches—one for boys, one for girls—and saw firsthand how the ministry was helping more than one hundred children, ages six to eighteen. John lived in a farmhouse at the boy's ranch with his wife, Tee, and his two children, Reagan and Brodie.

Each Big Oak Ranch was dotted with comfortable two-story brick houses, each home to a Christian couple and eight children who were offered love, discipline, and direction. The house parents chose a local church for the children to attend. Our children, Andrea and Patrick, fit right in and played with some of the kids on the ranch grounds, which was heartwarming to witness.

The children at Big Oak Boys' Ranch and Big Oak Girls' Ranch attended nearby Westbrook Christian School, where they made up one-fourth of the 400-member student body. John's children attended Westbrook as well.

We were there on a Thursday night in the fall, and our

family piled into John's van for a JV football game between Westbrook and another area school. Brodie, like my daughter Andrea, was a seventh grader, but he was the JV team's quarterback. That meant he was playing against high school freshmen and sophomores—kids two to three years older. That made for a big gap in physical size and maturity, especially since these were the puberty years.

I stood on the sidelines, amazed at the passing demonstration I saw. Brodie, who ran the offense out of the shotgun formation, threw every down, except when he was chased out of the pocket. His passing skills were impressive, and not just for someone his age; they would have been stunning for a high school senior five years older.

Brodie Croyle, if you know your Alabama football, went on to have a great college career as the Crimson Tide quarterback, wearing No. 12, the same number Alabama greats Joe Namath and Kenny Stabler had worn. The Kansas City Chiefs drafted Brodie, but he had a short, injury-plagued career, due mostly to playing behind a porous offensive line that allowed him to take too many hits. Brodie, married and the father of a son, retired after the 2011 season.

So why do I share this story?

Because John Croyle impacted my life and my kids' lives far more than watching football games at a stadium or on TV could have. But football was the avenue that brought us together. Football helped build the Big Oak Ranch, and the sacrifice and hard work John learned at the sound of Bear Bryant's whistle helped shape the lives of thousands of abused and abandoned kids over the past forty years.

Crimson Tide fans have a saying: Football isn't life or

death—it's far more important than that. Perhaps they have the right to gloat a bit since the University of Alabama won three of the four BCS national championships between 2010 and 2013—and look poised to win more titles as of this writing. But stories like John Croyle's remind me that the great game of football is not the end-all and be-all but a means to an end. That's the way it should be for a godly man like John. Perspective counts every time.

Besides that, who's playing this weekend?

SOURCE MATERIAL

Unless otherwise noted, all quotations are from interviews conducted between Mike Yorkey and the players and coaches.

Introduction
"The players wanted me to understand that apart from Sundays . . ." from "Are We Having Fun Yet?" by Stefan Fatsis, *Sports Illustrated*, July 14, 2008, and available at http://sportsillustrated.cnn.com/vault/article/magazine/MAG1141764/index.htm

1. Corey Lynch: Safety in God's Hands
"I don't want to pat myself on the back . . ." from "Tampa Bay Buccaneers Safety Corey Lunch a Hero in the Secondary," by Gary Shelton, *Tampa Bay Times*, December 11, 2010, and available at http://www.tampabay.com/sports/football/bucs/tampa-bay-buccaneers-safety-corey-lynch-a-hero-in-the-secondary/1139541

3. Andy Studebaker: Hands Off the Wheel
"We liked him, going back to his junior year when he had all those sacks . . ." from "YouTube Pushed Studebaker Up on NFL Draft Board," by Paul Domowitch, *Philadelphia Daily News*, May 22, 2008, and available at http://boards.philadelphiaeagles.com/topic/496534-eagles-youtube-pushed-studebaker-up-on-nfl-draft-board/

4. Jared Allen: Making Mincemeat of Quarterbacks

"Hunting is just peace, silent, a complete separation from the rest of the world . . ." from *The Quarterback Killer's Cookbook* by Jared Allen, GameDay Sports, 2010, page 5.

"You like those hamburger we ate the other night?" from *The Quarterback Killer's Cookbook* by Jared Allen, GameDay Sports, 2010, page 2.

"Okay, this is what you have to do, Bud . . ." from "Jared Allen Craves the Thrill of the Hunt," by Mike Nahrstedt, *The Sporting News*, June 13, 2008, and available at http://aol. sportingnews.com/nfl/story/2008-06-13/jared-allen-craves-thrill-hunt

"He's a very good football player, but a young man at risk . . ." from "Allen Suspended for Violating Substance Abuse Policy," by Len Pasquarelli, espn.com, April 27, 2007, and available at http://sports.espn.go.com/nfl/news/story?id=2851494

"I told him, 'You're screwing up this family's name . . . ,'" from "Born to Be Wild: Jared Allen Has Tried to Tone It Down, But There Are Limits," by Mark Emmons, *San Jose Mercury News*, and available at http://www.mercurynews.com/49ers/ci_8222779

"My answer was no . . ." from "NFL Award Winner Talks Faith and Football," by Tom Buehring, *The 700 Club*, and available at http://www.cbn.com/700club/features/amazing/TOM13_Jared_Allen.aspx

"When you think you're outnumbered, God's got your back . . ." from "NFL Award Winner Talks Faith and Football," by Tom Buehring, *The 700 Club*, and available at http://www.cbn.com/700club/features/amazing/TOM13_Jared_Allen.aspx

"I wanted to see if this guy was a con artist . . ." from "Vikings Won Over by Talents of 'Changed' Jared Allen," by Jim Corbett, *USA Today*, May 8, 2008, and available at http://usatoday30.usatoday.com/sports/football/nfl/vikings/2008-05-08-sw-jared-allen_N.htm

"They actually took one away from me in Green Bay. . ." from "Jared Allen: Sack Record Should Have Been Mine," by Jarrett Bell, USA Today, August 27, 2012, and available at http://content.usatoday.com/communities/thehuddle/post/2012/08/jared-allen-sack-record/1#.UPCGEaV9n8s

"It's like being runner-up at the prom . . ." from "Jared Allen Feels Like 'Runner-Up at the Prom' with Near-Sack Record," by Doug Farrar, *Yahoo Sports*, January 1, 2012, and available at http://sports.yahoo.com/nfl/blog/shutdown_corner/post/jared-allen-feels-like-runner-up-at-the-prom-with-near-sack-record?urn=nfl,wp15000

"Pass Rushing 101" is adapted from "Pass Rushing with Jared Allen, "by Scott Mackar, *Stack* magazine, March 1, 2008, and available at http://www.stack.com/2008/03/01/pass-rushing-with-jared-allen/

6. NFL Quarterbacks: The Highest Highs and the Lowest Lows

Drew Brees
"I'm very faith-driven in my life . . ." from "Marching In,"
by Tim Layden, *Sports Illustrated*, January 22, 2007, and
available at http://sportsillustrated.cnn.com/vault/article/
magazine/MAG1105608/3/index.htm

Colin Kaepernick
"It's not really a respect thing . . ." from "A Call Kaepernick
Should Make," by Rick Reilly, espn.com, January 30, 2013,
and available at http://espn.go.com/espn/story/_/id/8897116/
colin-kaepernick-birth-mom

Christian Ponder
"We tried to keep the attention away from us . . ." from
"Christian Ponder's Marriage to Samantha Steele No
Longer a Secret," by Chuck Schilken, *Los Angeles Times*,
December 19, 2012, and available at http://www.latimes.
com/sports/sportsnow/la-sp-sn-christian-ponder-samantha-
steele-20121219,0,1084051.story

Tony Romo
"I can easily pinpoint one time that stands out to me . . ." from
"Jason Witten & Tony Romo Testimony" from Prestonwood
Baptist Church and available on vimeo at http://vimeo.
com/20620940

Matt Ryan

"When asked how his faith intersects with sports . . ." from "Matt Ryan Talks Football, Faith to Douglasville Full House," by John Barker, *Douglasville Patch* online newspaper, December 5, 2012, and available at http://douglasville.patch.com/articles/matt-ryan-talks-football-faith-to-packed-douglasville-crowd#video-12454423

Russell Wilson

"More than anything, I think they [the Seattle coaching staff] saw how I prepared . . ." from "Russell Wilson Defied All Odds to Become the Talk of the NFL," by Danny O'Neil, *Seattle Times*, December 22, 2012, and available at http://seattletimes.com/html/seahawks/2019965454_wilson23.html?cmpid=2628

7. Greg Schiano: Coaching with Purpose

"Let me start with Eric LeGrand . . ." from *Believe: My Faith and the Tackle That Changed My Life* by Eric LeGrand with Mike Yorkey, William Morrow, New York, 2012, page 140.

"I came home the first day of double sessions . . ." from "Tampa Bay Buccaneers Coach Greg Schiano Rules with an Iron Fist," by Rick Stroud, *Tampa Bay Times*, September 7, 2012, and available at http://www.tampabay.com/sports/football/bucs/tampa-bay-buccaneers-coach-greg-schiano-rules-with-an-iron-fist/1250300

"I had no inkling . . ." from *Believe: My Faith and the Tackle That Changed My Life* by Eric LeGrand with Mike Yorkey, William Morrow, New York, 2012, page 237.

"I certainly understand why Coach . . ." from *Believe: My Faith and the Tackle That Changed My Life* by Eric LeGrand with Mike Yorkey, William Morrow, New York, 2012, page 243.

8. Terrell Fletcher: The Heart of a Chaplain

Police report information on Jovan Belcher from "Exclusive: Police Reports Detail Belcher, Perkins' Last Hours," by Christine Vendel, *Kansas City Star*, December 4, 2012, and available at http://www.kansascity.com/2012/12/04/3946159/belcher-shot-himself-as-kc-police.html

"One of the greatest needs women have is security . . ." from "Making the Tough Calls," by David A. Patten, *Newsmax* magazine, January 2009, and available at http://w3.newsmax.com/a/jan09/chaplains/

9. Two-Minute Warning: John Croyle of the Big Oak Ranch

"I teach these things . . ." from "Top 50 Quotes from Bear Bryant" from the Saturday Down South website, August 7, 2012, and available at http://www.saturdaydownsouth.com/2012/bear-bryant-50-quotes/